World Wisdom
The Library of Perennial Philosophy

The Library of Perennial Philosophy is dedicated to the exposition of the timeless Truth underlying the diverse religions. This Truth, often referred to as the *Sophia Perennis*—or Perennial Wisdom—finds its expression in the revealed Scriptures as well as in the writings of the great sages and the artistic creations of the traditional worlds.

Introduction to Hindu Dharma: Illustrated appears as one of our selections in the Spiritual Masters: East & West series.

Spiritual Masters: East & West Series

This series presents the writings of great spiritual masters of the past and present from both East and West. Carefully selected essential writings of these sages are combined with biographical information, glossaries of technical terms, historical maps, and pictorial and photographic art in order to communicate a sense of their respective spiritual climates.

Testimonies

"The two days we spent in his company will never be forgotten. There was pure spirituality."
—**Her Majesty Queen Frederika of Greece**

"The *Paramacharya* whom I considered as living sage of the contemporary world and the highest spiritual divinity will always remain the source of inspiration in the thoughts and deeds of the countless followers all over the world."
—**S.B. Thapa**, former Prime Minister of Nepal

"The greatest man of this century was the Acharya."
—**Dr. J.W. Elder**, Wisconsin University

"I remember very clearly that Indiraji got a lot of peace and inspiration meeting Parampujya Swami Chandrasekharji. I too have got the opportunity to meet him along with Rajivji. Kanchi has been considered as one of the most holy cities and has a very strong relationship with my family."
—**Smt. Sonia Gandhi**, President, Indian National Congress

"Before I went to India I had heard and read much about the great 'soul force' of its holy men and saints but I had assumed that this was something in the ancient past. And it was not until I had met Sankaracharya that I realized it was still part of the living force of Hinduism today."
—**Milton Singer**, University of Chicago

"When were we separate…? We are always together."
—**Ramana Maharshi**, speaking about the Jagadguru

"He interpreted *Sanatana Dharma* in such a way that it evoked pride towards our age-old tradition and also gave us a sense of direction to understand and meet modern India's challenges and problems."
—**Śri A.B. Vajpayee**, Former Prime Minister of India

"He had transcendent spirituality. He symbolized humankind's quest for the truth, peace, and harmony."
—**Dr. Shankar Dayal Sharma**, former President of India

"A great sage, one of the leading lights of the spiritual world."
—**Śri P. V. Narasimha Rao**, Former Prime Minister of India

"The *Paramacharya* is one of the greatest saints of our times. To be with him is always a great spiritual experience."
—**Dr. P.C. Alexander,** Governor of Maharashtra

"The greatness of His blessing was so immense that this human container was incapable of holding it without its overflowing which resulted as tears. Tears of utter fulfillment which washed away the container, causing it to dissolve, for a while, into the Reality He symbolizes."
—**Princess Irene of Greece**

உ

Sri Chandramouleeswaraya Namaha:

Sri Sankara Bhaghavadpadacharya Paramparagatha Moolamnaya Sarvagnapeeta :

His Holiness Sri Kanchi Kamakoti Peetadhipathi

JAGADGURU SRI SANKARACHARYA SWAMIGAL
SRIMATAM SAMSTHANAM

No. 1, Salai Street, Kanchipuram - 631 502. TamilNadu, India.

June 29, 2007

Sri Kanchi Kamakoti Peetam is happy to learn that World Wisdom – The Library of Perennial Philosophy is bringing out a series on the Spiritual Masters of the East and the West. Timeless Truth thus presented will enhance understanding and will go a long way in promoting harmony around the world.

We are pleased that World Wisdom will bring out a book called Introduction to Hindu Dharma: from Discourses by the 68th Acharya of Sri Kanchi Kamakoti Peetam, Jagadguru Sri Chandrasekharendra Saraswati Swamigal. The Acharya accepted 'Sanyasa Dharma' and became the Peetadhipathi of Sri Kanchi Kamakoti Peetam in 1907 – exactly a hundred years ago. This is the 'Peetarohana Shatabdi Mahotsava' year and has been celebrated in several parts of India and overseas. It is Divine will, that World Wisdom should bring out this volume in this Peetarohana Shatabdi Mahotsava year.

We are aware of the sincere commitment, dedication and devotion with which the preparation of this book has been approached. May the blessings of our Acharya be bestowed on everyone who has worked on this book and every one who reads the book. May this book inspire people to follow the path of 'Dharma'.

Narayana Smriti

Introduction to Hindu Dharma

Illustrated

Jagadguru His Holiness Sri Chandrasekharendra
Saraswati Swamigal, Sankaracharya of Kanchi
The 68th Acharya of Kanchi Kamakoti Peetam

Introduction by
Arvind Sharma

Edited by
Michael Oren Fitzgerald

World Wisdom

Introduction to Hindu Dharma: Illustrated

Book design by Susana Marín

Library of Congress Cataloging-in-Publication Data

Chandrasekharendra Saraswati, Jagatguru Sankaracharya of Kamakoti, 1893-1994.
[Selections. English. 2008]
Introduction to Hindu dharma : illustrated / Chandrasekharendra Saraswati ; introduction by Arvind Sharma ; edited by Michael Oren Fitzgerald.
p. cm.— (The library of perennial philosophy. Spiritual masters: East & West series)
Selected discourses.
Includes bibliographical references and index.
ISBN 978-1-933316-48-2 (pbk. : alk. paper) 1. Hinduism—Doctrines. I. Fitzgerald, Michael Oren, 1949- II. Title.
BL1212.76.C485 2008
294.5'48—dc22

2007044697

Printed on acid-free paper in China.

For information address World Wisdom, Inc.
P.O. Box 2682, Bloomington, Indiana 47402-2682
www.worldwisdom.com

Contents

Preface

When His Holiness the 68th Jagadguru of Kanchi died in 1994 at the age of 100, he was one of the most beloved and honored spiritual figures of the twentieth century in India and much of Asia and Europe. But despite high praise from kings and prime ministers, he remains virtually unknown in the West. This book therefore has the distinction of introducing both the sage and his spiritual legacy to the Western world in the form of an irreplaceable introduction to Hinduism[1] in today's world.

The Jagadguru is known by other names, including Śankarāchārya, or great teacher of the Śankara tradition.[2] Śankara was one of the most important philosophers and spiritual teachers in the history of India. According to tradition, Śankara was born in the state of Kerala in 509 B.C. and lived for 32 years. It is incontrovertible that Śankara was one of the greatest philosophers in the history of India and in his short life he made a profound and lasting impact on the subsequent life of India. He both firmly established a major philosophical school of thought, known as *Advaita Vedānta* (non-dualism), and also breathed new life into Vedic tradition, which ultimately became known as Hinduism. During his life Śankara established five major *āśrams* (*pīthas*) throughout India, each of which is the seat of a Śankarāchārya—a continuous living representative of Śankara's school of thought. The Jagadguru is therefore the 68th in a line of great teachers (*āchāryas*) from Kanchi who can trace their spiritual lineage directly back to the founder of this school of thought.

His Holiness Jagadguru Śri Chandrasekharendra Sarasvati Swamigal was installed at the tender age of 13 as the pontiff in Kanchi of the hallowed line of succession back to Ādhi Śankara; thus more than 87 years of his life was dedicated to preserving and perpetuating traditional Hindu dharma (code of conduct).[3]

In the last century a handful of gurus from India have become well known in the West who presented Hindu teachings that focused on prayer and spiritual virtues. For example, the Sanskrit term *mantra* has found its way into our parlance (a *mantra* is technically a sacred formula that is constantly repeated as a means of invocatory prayer), and we understand that one goal of Eastern religions, including Hinduism, is to lead devout renunciates to Self-realization or a direct connection with God.

Western readers have also had access to the metaphysical teachings of the great philosopher teachers throughout the history of India, but the primary texts of the various metaphysi-

---

[1] There is no term for Hinduism in the traditional vocabulary. The word for Hinduism used by the Jagadguru is *sanātana dharma*, or eternal and universal code of conduct.

[2] His formal name is Pūjyaśrī Chandra Śekharendra Sarasvatī Swāmī. He is the *āchārya* (great teacher) of the Kānchi Kāmakoti Pītha. There are five *pīthas* in different locations throughout India that were originally established by Ādhi Śankara. Each *pītha* is the seat of a religious and spiritual head with its own line of succession. Śri Chandrasekharendra Saraswati was the 68th Śankarāchārya in the line of succession of the Kānchi Pītham.

At the time Śankara created these *pīthas*, he formulated a specific code of conduct detailing how people who live or work in the *pīthas* (*pīthapadhis*) must conduct themselves. A *pītha* and an *āśram* are physically similar because each is an abode of ascetics or *sannyāsins*. It is Śankara's specific code of conduct that differentiates a *pītha* from what is commonly known in the West as an *āśram*.

[3] HH the Jagadguru was born at Villupuram on 20th May, 1894.

cal schools of thought are difficult to understand without the benefit of an interpretation that necessarily simplifies the underlying concepts. Most gurus known in the West have not chosen to enter into the realm of metaphysical explanations. Scholars have done their best to explain complex philosophical concepts, but these explanations are, in varying degrees, from the outside looking in. They are not from the mouth of a person who is widely acknowledged as already having achieved Self-realization and whose very *dharma* is to act as a primary representative for traditional Hinduism in today's world. The words of the Jagadguru come from this vantage point.[4]

Hinduism is not just for those who renounce the world to lead an austere life of prayer—it is also a way of life that supported an entire civilization for almost three millennia. But during the twentieth century well established aspects of the Hindu tradition have been drawn into outright disfavor, such as the idea of a caste system. Almost no one in the West has stepped forward to present an integral understanding of the conflicts between Hindu tradition and modernity, until now.

The discourses in this book cover all three categories of teaching: prayer and virtue; an explanation of Hindu metaphysical Truth; and an explanation of the conflict between traditional Hindu *dharma* and modernity. Upon review of this ambitious agenda one might conclude that this is a complex technical treatise. In order to understand why such a conclusion is not accurate, it is necessary to understand the context in which these discourses were first delivered.

The home of the Jagadguru is his *āśram* (*pītha*), which is in the southern state of Tamil Nadu. The Jagadguru did not write, but rather used the traditional oral method of teaching, which requires that the guru be physically present with his admirers to impart his teaching.[5] The physical presence of the guru is also required because many of his devotees do not read. In the modern world it is exceedingly difficult for his admirers to leave their families, homes, and jobs to spend extended time at his *āśram*. Therefore, each year he travels throughout South India and "camps" for weeks or even months at a time in locations that are accessible to his devotees from each area. The Śankarāchārya and his entourage literally live in tents and erect a portable platform that elevates him during his discourses and ritual observances so that he can be seen by the multitudes that come to see and hear him.

During his discourses he typically speaks in Tamil, the main language of the region; but he frequently uses Sanskrit terms because it is essential for his audience to have a basic understanding of the sacred language that is the source of the Hindu revelation. The Jagadguru's mission and function applies to one and all; thus, his audience comes from all walks of life—from governmental ministers to manual laborers and peasants. In order for his audience to follow his discourses he balances the need to simplify his message with the need to communicate a precise understanding of his words and concepts. One method he employs is to frequently translate Sanskrit terms into Tamil during his discourses.

---

[4] There are hundreds, indeed thousands, of recorded statements from prominent people, including saints such as Ramana Maharshi, which testify that H.H. the 68th Jagadguru of Kanchi was a Self-realized person.

[5] The word *upa-ni-shad* means "sit near by". The Jagadguru has said that "The Upanishads (Hindu scripture) are teachings imparted by a guru to his student sitting by his side [or at his feet]." Many of the greatest spiritual masters of Hinduism have only employed such oral teachings, although in our day their disciples have painstakingly recorded, transcribed, and translated their words in order to preserve and communicate this wisdom to a wider audience.

I have selected this text from the more than 6,500 pages of his discourses that have been recorded, transcribed, and translated into English.[6] In many instances the Jagadguru's own Tamil definitions for Sanskrit terms have been translated into English. I have retained these definitions and incorporated additional definitions into the text to facilitate reader comprehension without constant recourse to a glossary.[7] To a large extent this follows the actual practice of the Jagadguru. Those readers willing to expend extra effort to understand some of his Sanskrit terminology will gain a deeper understanding of the Śankarāchārya's message.

For more than seventy years, devotees who included royalty and street sweepers sat at the feet of the Jagadguru to hear his wisdom. His discourses covered every important question in life. Whenever he camped in one spot for an extended time he changed the subject of his discourse from day to day in order to cumulatively present an integral understanding of all facets of his message to his diverse audience. Those disciples who wanted to gain a greater understanding of the Śankarāchārya's message spent more time sitting at his feet. The editing process for this book has attempted to recreate the experience of sitting near the guru every day during a camping period of between one to two weeks.[8] It is evident that this is a simplification of his entire message, but it is intended that these selections will provide an introduction to the Jagadguru's essential message and point interested readers to further study. This constitutes a unique introduction to Hindu *dharma* from the voice of the person who millions of people acknowledge was one of the greatest representatives of Hinduism in the twentieth century.

* * *

The voice of the Jagadguru is an essential part of his message. But Hindus believe that the guru's presence is also part of his message because his spiritual presence can be felt by sincere spiritual seekers. Photographs cannot convey the entirety of the guru's spiritual presence, but they can give readers additional insight into the character of the *Mahā-svāmi* (great swami), as he is called by his devotees. The original photographs of the Jagadguru come from his *āśram* in Kanchi, but they have been painstakingly restored by World Wisdom.[9] The photographs of the Śankarāchārya are from all phases of his life.

---

[6] I am grateful to both the 69th Pontiff His Holiness Śri Jayendra Saraswati Swamigal and the 70th Pontiff His Holiness Śri Sankara Vijayendra Saraswati Swamigal, of Kānchi Kāmakoti Pītha without whose approvals the project could not have taken place. I am also grateful to Pujya Śri Mettur Swamigal with whom I had initially discussed the project when I was in Kanchi and to Śri. V. Krishnamachari for his valuable suggestions and his meticulous proofing of the manuscript.

[7] In my editing process I have retained all of the Jagadguru's own definitions for Sanskrit terms and I have repeated some definitions in different places. The editor's and translator's insertions are shown in parentheses. I also eliminated many Sanskrit terms, leaving only his English translation of the word, and eliminated most Sanskrit phrases and sentences, such as the names of various books and scriptures, either replacing them with phrases that describe the reference or moving the reference into endnotes.

[8] Taking into consideration all of the aforementioned simplifications of Sanskrit terminology to adjust for Western readers.

[9] When we first visited the Kānchi Kāmakoti Pītha in January 2004 we saw many old photographs of the Jagadguru that were in need of restoration and preservation. After discussions with officials from the *pītha*, a procedure was developed for representatives of the *pītha* to send photographs to World Wisdom via express courier. The old photographs were scanned and restored and then the originals were returned to the *pītha*, together with digital files and enlarged sepia prints using archival inks on archival paper. Once the procedure was successfully tested, the *pītha*

It is axiomatic that the sacred art of India is inextricably linked to its spirituality. It is helpful to put the faces of statuary behind the respective names of some of the different gods and goddesses referenced by the Jagadguru. Most of the other photographic selections are of sacred places associated with the Jagadguru or places he has referenced in the text. We intend that the illustrations will provide a taste of the spiritual perfume of the Hindu tradition.

* * *

India is a home to many vibrant religions and the only country that is a birthplace of several major religions.[10] While there is obvious tension between India and Pakistan, in part because of an ongoing border dispute, there is remarkably little trouble between the adherents to different religions and members of different Hindu schools within India. Perhaps one reason for the largely peaceful coexistence of so many religions and sects is a general recognition of the existence of one, all-powerful God Who is the underlying Source of all manifestation, including every religious form. The Jagadguru referred to this aspect of the Godhead as the *Paramātman*, while Frithjof Schuon, the late Swiss philosopher, coined the phrase "transcendent Unity of religion" to refer to this same principle.[11] When traveling through India, one often hears people of different beliefs and diverse economic backgrounds repeat a phrase that has a similar meaning: "many forms—only one God."[12] The Jagadguru's explanations throughout this text provide great clarity to this concept, to say the least.

An integral understanding of the Śankarāchārya's metaphysical philosophy—that there is one timeless Truth underlying diverse religious forms and that each of those forms constitutes a valid path to the same God—can therefore be the basis for a true interfaith dialogue. The difficulty of interfaith dialogue is to look past the outward differences in the forms of the religions and to carefully examine the shared inner truths. Discernment between the essential and the non-essential forms of spirituality is therefore an indispensable element in interfaith dialogue. This search for common truths can provide important understandings that can deepen each person's own faith, while also providing a more profound appreciation for the beliefs and spiritual practices of other people. The Jagadguru's message provides keys to this search.

Michael Oren Fitzgerald

---

sent additional shipments of old photographs and the process was repeated. All costs for this service were paid by World Wisdom.

[10] India is the birth place of Hinduism, Buddhism, and Jainism. Twenty-five percent of the population of the state of Kerala is Christian, in large part because it is the final home of one of the Christ's original disciples, Saint Thomas. India is the home of one of the great flowerings of the Muslim world. Even after the partition with Pakistan, more Muslims live in India than in the entire Arabian Peninsula. The Zoroastrians who fled Iran after the coming of Islam found welcome sanctuary in India and the Sikh faith is also centered in India.

[11] In the text I have paraphrased Schuon's definition of the transcendent Unity of religion to succinctly define the term *Paramātman*. Schuon's writings provide keys to identify the same essential inner truths within each religion—without which religion does not exist—and explain how the outward differences in the forms of the religions are not essential, but rather vary so as to accentuate different Divine characteristics.

[12] This comment is true with respect to the forms of the different religions and also with respect to only Hinduism, where many manifestations of One God have given rise to different forms of worship.

Introduction

I was shown a clock which stopped ticking right at the very moment the 68th Jagadguru of Kanchi, popularly known as the Paramācārya, dropped his body at the age of one hundred, when I visited Kanchi around the turn of the century. Clocks stop but not time. So when I was invited to write an introduction to the teachings and preachings of His Holiness Śri Chandrasekharendra Saraswati Swamigal, for such was his full name and title, I was happy to accept the request. It was a singular honor to be asked to do so, for it is difficult not to be moved by the spontaneous expressions of esteem the very mention of his name elicited almost universally.

This book is therefore that rare commodity—a book about Hinduism by a prominent Hindu of our times, who also stands in a line of disciplic succession[1] traceable to Śaṅkara himself, the famous figure often called *ādhi* or the first Śaṅkarācārya, to distinguish him from those who bear his name as a title.[2] The range of achievements he is said to have compressed into the unbelievably short life of thirty-two years is nothing short of astonishing. His systemization of *Advaita Vedānta* as a philosophical school set it on a trajectory which culminated in its becoming a major, if not the major, school of Hindu thought, a status it continues to enjoy to this day. It also includes, (paradoxically) the validation of the "six cults" usually associated with Ganeśa, Sūrya, Viṣṇu, Śiva, Śakti, and Kumāra, earning him the designation of *ṣaṇmatasthāpacācārya*.[3] I put "paradoxically" in parentheses because while historically he is regarded as the validator of these cults, philosophically he is associated with the school of *Advaita Vedānta* according to which the ultimate reality is best described as one which is not only free from cultic but any attributes whatever (*nirguṇa brahma*). While this might appear paradoxical to the outsider of the tradition, it is perfectly logical for the insider to the tradition, familiar with the tradition's penchant for promoting the availability of religious ideas (to annex the title of a book) to as many people as possible. A similar convergence is reflected in Paramācārya's position with that of Ādhi Śaṅkara in terms of social reform,[4] who, according to a tradition preserved in Kerala, the land of his birth, is credited with having abolished the practice of Satī.[5] After all, in the spiritual economy of *Advaita Vedānta*, it is the mind which has to be killed and not the body. The Paramācārya inveighed against dowry (pp. 39, 97) in

[1] The term *disciplic* (from disciple) does not appear in the dictionaries I consulted, but may have to be used on the analogy of "apostolic succession" in Christian circles in order to refer to the *guru-paramparā* (disciplic succession) in Hinduism.

[2] See William Cenkner, *A Tradition of Teachers: Śaṅkara and the Jagadgurus Today* (Delhi: Motilal Banarsidass, 1983). Readers disposed to question the current chronological framework of Hindu Studies should note that the Paramācārya had his own views in the matter. He places the birth of Ādhi Śaṅkara, who is assigned by most scholars to around the eighth century A.D., in 509 B.C. on the basis of his own calculations, explained in detail in his collected works in Tamil.

[3] S. Radhakrishnan, *Eastern Religions and Western Thought* (second edition) (London: Oxford University Press, 1940), p. 311.

[4] See S. Radhakrishnan, *The Brahma Sūtra: The Philosophy of Spiritual Life* (London: George Allen & Unwin Ltd., 1960), p. 37 note 1.

[5] P.V. Kane, *History of Dharmaśāstra* (Poona: Bhandarkar Oriental Research Institute, 1974), Vol. II Pt. I, p. 506.

the same reformist spirit and it is interesting to speculate how he might have reacted to the current practice of feticide, which is currently skewing the sex ratio in India. It is difficult to second-guess saints. But one wouldn't be surprised if he would have dubbed it *devīhatyā* or the killing of a goddess (thereby creating the word Devicide as a new take on deicide). Many tend to hold tradition responsible for such sex-selection but the tenor of his remarks in this book suggests he might have held modernity equally if not solely culpable, for if there is any practice virtually universally opposed within classical Hinduism, outside of the *sādhāraṇa dharmas* or norms common for all human beings, it is abortion.[6]

I described Paramācārya as a contemporary exponent of Hinduism but I could well have been rapped on the knuckles by him for using the term Hinduism to refer to a religious tradition he would preferably describe as *sanātana dharma*[7] or the eternal and universal code of conduct. The inadequacies associated with the word "Hinduism" have also been noted by others (sometimes even Western scholars)[8] which ultimately remains an outsider's designation (though internalized by now to a large extent by "Hindus"). Unlike them, however, the Paramācārya draws a radical conclusion from the nomenclatural anonymity of the Hindu tradition,[9] namely, that it has no name for itself because once it was the only religion around and "when there is only one, where is the problem of identifying it" (p. 13). Other religions came into play when it ceased to be the only game in town, as it were. Other religions arose when it began to languish in other parts of the world, while in India it maintained its continuity. The word to be used for it in this new situation should be *sanātana dharma*, which possesses such distinctive features as the doctrine of karma and rebirth, or the belief that "the one and only *Paramātman* who has neither a form nor attributes is manifested in different forms with attributes" (p. 14), a belief sometimes unfortunately confused with idolatry (p. 14).

The Paramācārya's presentation of Hindu *dharma* is remarkable for its convergences and divergences with its presentation by another great Acharya or teacher of our times, that Acharya of non-violence—Mahatma Gandhi. The coincidence of their positions on opposition to conversion, either from or to a religion, is uncanny (see pp. 8, 11, 16, 29). Nevertheless, he adduces an argument in support of his position which was never used by Mahatma Gandhi to the best of my knowledge, that although Hinduism contains a plethora of rituals, "yet its canonical texts do not contain any rite for conversion" (p. 8). He, however, would not censure those who convert people to their faith (p. 11), although Mahatma Gandhi would not hesitate to do so. The Paramācārya and Mahatma Gandhi also share an opposition to machinery (p. 27, 29), modernity (p. 39), and a lack of such opposition to the "caste system", which they view as a sheet anchor against the viciousness of economic competition (pp. 25, 103).

---

[6] Julius Lipner, "The Classical Hindu View on Abortion and the Moral Status of the Unborn", in Harold J. Coward, Julius J. Lipner and Katherine K. Young, *Hindu Ethics: Purity, Abortion, Euthanasia* (Albany, N.Y.: State University of New York Press, 1989), pp. 41-69.

[7] For a discussion of the various significations of the term see Arvind Sharma, *Modern Hindu Thought: An Introduction* (New Delhi: Oxford University Press, 2005), pp. 94-105.

[8] Wilfred Cantwell Smith, *The Meaning and End of Religion* (New York: The Macmillan Company, 1963), pp. 63-65.

[9] This dimension of Paramācārya's thought is highlighted in R. Balasubramaniam, "Two Contemporary Exemplars of the Hindu Tradition: Ramaṇa Maharṣi and Śri Candraśekharendra Sarasvati", in Krishna Sivaraman, ed., *Hindu Spirituality: Vedas Through Vedānta* (New York: Crossroad, 1989), pp. 381-382.

Both also felt that one should pursue one's hereditary vocation (p. 103) in order to ensure socio-economic harmony. Towards the end of his life, however, Mahatma Gandhi had started speaking in favor of a casteless society, as a way of eliminating the negative dimensions of caste but Paramācārya's solution was to restore the system to its pristine purity by calling upon Brahmins to revert to a pure life style, departure from which on their part had, he argued, by a kind of domino effect, led to its perversion in the first place (p. 26). Thus both Paramācārya and the so-called reformists believe in reform—but of different kinds. It is interesting though that he looks forward to a future in which "everyone should be able to perform Vedic rites himself" (p. 30) without the help of priests. Another issue on which they differ, after a point, is the desirability of non-violence. The Paramācārya, unlike Gandhi, seems more willing to accept exceptions to non-violence as "in the case of a righteous or just war and in sacrifice" (p. 123), where, by sacrifice, sacrificial ritual is meant. Another major point on which he differs from Mahatma Gandhi is the role accorded to conscience as a source of *dharma*. Conscience was the ultimate court of appeal for Mahatma Gandhi, but for Paramācārya it was too subjective in nature to play that role. He feared that it would throw the door wide open to random moral relativism, a danger recognized by Mahatma Gandhi, by the way. Hence Gandhi's insistence on leading a pure moral life, to prevent the voice of conscience from becoming the ventriloquist to our own desires.

A good portion of the book is addressed to social issues, like the caste system and the position of women. These sections are helpful in clarifying the traditional perspective, specially on the position of Brahmins and of women. The Paramācārya states on the first point: "A wrong notion has gained currency that in the *Varṇāśrama* system the Brahmin enjoys more comforts than others, and that he has more income…" (p. 105). He then details the regimen of the Brahmin's life in some detail. The initial tendency might be to dismiss it as apologetics but the evidence possesses considerable weight. Hunger seems to have been the professional hazard of a practicing Brahmin. Substance to this position is lent by what otherwise seems to be a point of (perhaps useless) minutiae—the difference in the connotation of the words *uncha* and *śila*, translated in English as "gleaning" and "picking". The Brahmin is supposed to ideally live by "gleaning" (*uncha*) and "picking" (*śila*) (*Manusmṛti* IV.5), and must never follow a worldly occupation for the sake of livelihood (*Manusmṛti* IV.11). Patrick Olivelle provides a note on the distinction between "gleaning" and "picking" as follows:

> *Gleaning and picking*: Gleaning (*uncha*), according to the traditional explanation, is gathering up ears of corn that have fallen on the ground when farmers take their harvest to their homes or granaries. Picking (*śila*) is gathering up ears of corn that have fallen to the ground from the plants in the field either before or after the harvest. The major difference is that the former is collected along the road and the latter in the field.[10]

[10] Patrick Olivelle, *The Law Code of Manu* (New York: Oxford University Press), 2004, pp. 248-249.

This is identified in the text as one of the ways in which the Vedic graduate is supposed to support himself! No wonder the *Manusmṛti* contains several references to the famished Brahmin.[11]

If the Paramācārya's position is in accord with facts, then how come they have gone virtually unreported, not to say unappreciated, for so long? It seems this point has suffered obscuration in the past because of the emphasis placed on (1) the advantages *secular* Brahmins may have enjoyed in society and (2) the privileged legal position Brahmins occupy in classical criminal law, and such obscuration has resulted in obfuscation. This has generated the impression that the Brahmins were living off the lard of the land. It must be noted, regarding the second point, that they do enjoy legal privileges but—and here the first point kicks in—it is not certain that secular Brahmins could enjoy them. A.L. Basham writes:

> Opinions differed as to whether a brāhmaṇ engaged in a secular profession was worthy of the respect accorded to the practicing member of his class, and no clear ruling is laid down. Manu, the most authoritative of the Smṛtis, is uncertain on this point, and in different parts of the text diametrically opposed views are given. As far as can be gathered from general literature the special rights of the brāhmaṇ were usually only granted to those who lived by sacrifice and teaching. Cārudatta, the poor brāhmaṇ hero of the play "The Little Clay Cart", receives scurvy treatment at the hands of the court, probably because he is a brāhmaṇ by birth only, and not by profession.[12]

So it is the economically underprivileged Brahmin who ends up legally privileged. The point has been missed because Western scholarship has focused on the Brahmin's privileges and indigenous presentations on the Brahmin's privations. The Paramācārya for instance, only focuses on the latter, although it is now possible to take a more comprehensive view of the allegedly privileged position of the Brahmin in the light of the argument presented by him.

The Paramācārya also argues that although women and *śūdras* were not eligible for certain sacraments in classical Hinduism, this does *not* mean that their position was generally low. He argues in fact for a higher status for them in the *Kali-yuga*. On this he is on solid ground.[13] But once again the situation turns out to be more complex. It is generally (but not universally) the position within classical Hinduism that women and *śūdras* do not undergo the investiture ceremony, to take a case in point. Now this fact is depicted as an *exclusion* in the *smṛti* texts but as an *exemption* in the Puranic texts. Paramācārya's account helps focus on the view that the apparent denial came to be treated as an exemption at certain times or in certain circles, and it is good to know that such was the case. One cannot however ignore the fact that it is also treated as an exclusion, at certain times and in certain texts. Once again Western accounts tend to focus on the *exclusion*, and the indigenous on the *exemption*.

It is a major accomplishment of the Paramācārya's account of Hinduism in this book that it remedies the discussion of ethics in the context of the Hindu tradition in a refreshing way. Hindu ethics has often been accused of being particularistic but Paramācārya points out

---

[11] See *Manusmṛti* IV.33-34; VII.133-134; X.105-108; XI.21.

[12] A.L. Basham, *The Wonder That Was India* (New Delhi: Rupa & Co., 1999), p. 140.

[13] P.V. Kane, *History of Dharmaśāstra*, Vol. V, Pt. II (second edition), pp. 928-929.

that this view is seriously flawed and in fact turns what is Hinduism's unique "asset" into a devastating "liability". He points out that "other religions lay down only such duties as are common to all their followers. In the Vedic religion there are two types of *dharma*, the one being common to all and the other to individual *varnas* (castes)" (p. 21).

This single ray of light can dispel a darkness which has lain over the study of Hinduism, or *sanātana dharma*, for two centuries. For a long time now it has been accepted as self-evident that Hindu ethics is particularistic and not even some very well-known Indologists have been able to avoid falling into this trap. It is in some ways a tempting thesis—from a Western perspective. Early observers, beginning with the Portuguese who gave us the word "caste", saw Hindu society as consisting of different natal groups with their own norms and practices. When the British took over and began to administer Hindu law, they focused on texts such as the *Manusmṛti*, which seemed specially concerned with delineating the different duties of the different *varṇas* or *jātis*. It soon became the dominant view that Hindu ethics is particularistic, a view baptized into sociology by Max Weber (1864-1920) and canonized by Louis Dumont (1911-1998). To the extent that the British did follow a policy of divide and rule (taking their cue from the Romans whose role they sought to emulate) it was in British interest to emphasize the disparate particularities of Indian and specially Hindu society and polity. The cumulative thrust of anthropology, philology, and imperialism buttressed the view that Hindu ethics was particularistic, a view which also then came to be fortified through the comparative study of religions and civilizations. Such particularism could then be identified as the hallmark of Hindu civilization, and then contrasted with the universalism of the Abrahamic religions, as well as the individualism of Western civilization in general.

There is only one problem with this view. It misses the point, which may be made as follows following the Paramācārya. Hinduism is characterized by a full recognition of *both* particularistic and universal ethics, so the difference between it and other religions and cultures consists *not* in the claim that it possesses *only* particularistic ethics, but rather that it possesses *both*, while other religions and cultures focus mostly or solely on the universal. Some academics have made this point but Paramācārya seems to be the first scholar-saint from within the tradition to state this position with clarity and vigor.

One might wish in conclusion to refer to a point made by the Paramācārya about the concept of the secular state in relation to India. He writes:

> We are called a "secular state". It means, we are told, a state that does not concern itself with matters of religion. It further means that the government can interfere only in social matters and not in religious affairs. But ours is a religion in which all aspects of life, individual and social, are woven together. So the laws enacted by the state to govern social life have an impact on our religion too. Our rulers do not recognize or accept this fact. They limit their view of religion to certain matters and think that all else belongs to the social sphere and are (*sic*) the concern of the government. In spite of its claim to being secular, the government thinks it fit to interfere with anything that has to do with the Hindu traditions.

Some of these inner contradictions of Indian secularism have only become magnified since he pinpointed them. We find here an anticipation of the concepts of "pseudo-secularism" and "asymmetrical secularism", which has provided the intellectual basis of the rise to political power by the Hindu right in recent years. Such forces are in eclipse at the moment but the reality portrayed by the Paramācārya has not changed for the better. His position in the matter articulates a danger regarding the Indian situation expressed by an academic as follows:

> If the state deals with the religion of a minority, there are definite political checks which will tend to limit the extent of the interference. When Hindu legislators and administrators deal with their own religion, that of the majority, there are no such checks. State interference in Hindu temples has been limited somewhere by the judiciary's interpretation of article 26 of the Constitution, but it is still very extensive. What is almost totally lacking is the consideration that the concept of the secular state itself imposes certain definite limitations on the functions of government. Not everything that needs to be done should be done by the state.[14]

The appeal of the book is not limited to the originality of some of its ideas but also rests on the felicity of its style. It is interspersed with quotable quotes: "The *Purāṇās* are the magnifying glass of the Vedas" (p. 69); "The restrictions must not be too many. There must be restriction on restrictions" (p. 76); "Those who complain that women have no right to perform sacrifices on their own must remember that men too have no right to the same without a wife" (p. 95); "Our affection for our wife, children, and others is in fact affection for ourselves" (p. 111); "[The problem then is]: Our love for others ends in sorrow. However, if there is no love there is no meaning in life" (p. 132); "True love knows neither reason nor motive" (p. 132). There is also this charming citation from Avvai: "There is no deceit that is hidden from the heart (mind)" (p. 41), and a metaphor from Rāmalinga Swamigal as a warning against forcing the pace of spiritual development, which might result in "prematurely ripe and withered fruit droppings" (p. 83).

With these words I would like to invite the reader to move on, from reading this introduction to the book, to the book itself.

Arvind Sharma
McGill University

[14] Donald Eugene Smith, *India as a Secular State* (Princeton, New Jersey: Princeton University Press, 1963), p. 497.

Religion in General

Dharma Alone Protects

You must look upon the world as belonging to the Lord, and it is your duty to so conduct yourself as to conform to this belief. This constitutes the *dharma* (code of conduct, set of duties) of humanity. Acts dictated solely by selfish interests will push one into unrighteousness. A man must learn to be less and less selfish in his thoughts and actions; he must always remember the Lord and must ever be conscious that He is the master of all this world. This view is the basis on which all religions have evolved.

No religion teaches us to live according to our whims and fancies; no religion asks us to acquire wealth and property for our personal needs alone. If a man believes that he alone is important, that he is all, he will live only for himself. That is why all religions speak of an entity called God and teach man to efface his ego or I-feeling. "Child," they tell him, "you are nothing before that Power, the author of this universe. It is He—that Power—who has endowed you with intelligence. Your intelligence, your intellect, must guide you on the path of *dharma*, righteousness. For this purpose you must look up to this Power for support." The great importance attached to *bhakti* or devotion in all religions is founded on this belief, the need for divine support for virtuous conduct.

Ordinarily it is not easy to develop faith in, or devotion to, God expressed in abstract terms. For the common people devotion must take the form of practical steps. That is how ritual originated. *Sandhyāvandana* (morning and evening prayers), *namāz* (Persian word for Islamic prayers) and other forms of prayer are examples of such ritual. The religions teach people their duties, how they must conduct themselves in this world, and how they must devote themselves to God in the very midst of their worldly life.

"Love everyone." "Live a life of sacrifice." "Serve mankind." Such are the teachings of the various religions. If a man lives according to these tenets, it is believed that his soul will reach God after it departs from his body. Those who subscribe to *Advaita* or non-dualism declare that the soul will become one with the Godhead. According to another system of belief, after reaching the Lord, the soul will serve Him and ever remain happy as the recipient of His compassion. There is no need to quarrel over the nature of the final state. "By following one path or another we attain the Lord. And that will be the end of all our sorrows, all our frustrations, and all our failures in this world. There will now be nothing but bliss, full and everlasting." No more than this do we need to know for the present.

If the *Paramātman* (Transcendent Unity of God—the Great Transcendent Self) is to draw us unto Himself we must, without fail, perform our duties to Him as well as to the world. It is these duties that constitute what is called *dharma*. *Dharma* it is that serves us when we dwell in our body and when we cease to dwell in it. It serves us in life and after life. When we are in this world we must do that which would take us to a desirable state after we depart from it. We take an insurance policy so that our relatives will be able to take care of themselves when we are gone. But is it not far more important to ensure that we will be happy in our afterlife? *Dharma* is afterlife insurance. But in this life too it is *dharma* that gives us peace and happiness.

There need be no doubt or confusion about the *dharma* we ought to follow. We are all steeped in the *dharma* that our great men have pursued from generation to generation. They have inwardly realized eternal beatitude and we know for certain that they lived without any care, unlike people in our own gen-

eration who are always discontented and are embroiled in agitations and demonstrations of all kinds. All we need to do is to follow the *dharma* that they practiced. If we tried to create a new *dharma* for ourselves it might mean trouble and all the time we would be torn by doubts as to whether it would bring us good or whether it would give rise to evil. It is best for us to follow the *dharma* practiced by the great men of the past, the *dharma* of our forefathers.

Man is subject to all kinds of hardships and misfortunes. To remind ourselves of this, we eat the bitter flowers of the neem on New Year's Day—that is, on the very first day of the year we accept the bitternesses of life. During the Pongal ceremony, which is celebrated almost towards the close of the year, we have sugarcane to chew. If we have only sweetness in the beginning we may have to experience bitterness towards the end. We must not have any aversion for the bitter but welcome it as the medicine administered by Mother Nature or by *dharma*. If we do so, in due course, we will learn to regard any experience, even if it be unpleasant, as a sweet one.

Dharma—and *dharma* alone—is our protecting shield.

One's religion is nothing but the *dharma* practiced by one's forefathers. May all adhere to their *dharma* with unwavering faith and courage and be rewarded with everlasting bliss.

Punya (Virtuous Action)

Nobody wants to be known as a sinner, but all the same we keep transgressing the bounds of morality and disobeying the divine law. We wish to enjoy the fruits of virtue without being morally good and without doing anything meritorious.

Arjuna says to Bhagavān Krishna (Lord Krishna): "No man wants to commit sin. Even so, Krishna, he does evil again and again. What is it that drives him so?" The Lord replies: "It is desire. Yes, it is desire, Arjuna."

Only by banishing desire from our hearts may we remain free from sin. How is it done? We cannot but be performing our works. Even when we are physically inactive, our mind remains active. All our mental and bodily activity revolves round our desires. And these desires thrust us deeper and deeper into sin. Is it, then, possible to remain without doing any work? Human nature being what it is, the answer is "No".

"It is difficult to quell one's thinking nor is it easy to remain without doing anything," says Tāyumānavā-svamigal (*swami*). We may stop doing work with the body, but how do we keep the mind quiet? The mind is never still. Apart from being unstill itself, it incites the body to action.

We are unable either to efface our desires or to cease from all action. Does it then mean that liberation is beyond us? Is there no way

out of the problem? Yes, there is. It is not necessary that we should altogether stop our actions in our present immature predicament. But, instead of working for our selfish ends, we ought to be engaged in such work as would bring benefits to the world as well as to our inward life. The more we are involved in such work, the less we shall be drawn by desire. This will to some extent keep us away from sin and at the same time enable us to do more meritorious work. We must learn the habit of doing work without any selfish motive. Work done without any desire for the fruits thereof is *punya*, or virtuous action.

We sin in four different ways. With our body we do evil; with our tongue we speak untruth; with our mind we think evil; and with our money we do so much that is wicked. We must learn to turn these very four means of evil into instruments of virtue.

We must serve others with our body and circumambulate the Lord and prostrate ourselves before him. In this way we earn merit. How do we use our tongue to add to our stock of virtue? By saying, by repeating, the names of the Lord. You will perhaps excuse yourself saying: "All our time is spent in earning our livelihood. How can we then think of God or repeat His Names?" A householder has a family to maintain; but is he all the time working for it? How much time does he waste in gossip, in amusements, in speaking ill of others, in reading the papers? Can't he spare a few moments to remember the Lord? He need not set apart a particular hour of the day for his *japa* (recitation of a *mantra*—a Divine formula). He may think of God even on the bus or the train as he goes to his office or any other place. Not a penny is he going to take with him finally after his lifelong pursuit of money. The Lord's name, Bhagavan *nāma*, is the only current coin in the other world.

The mind is the abode of *Īśvara* (the *Paramātman* with attributes) but we make a rubbish can of it. We must cleanse it, install the Lord in it and be at peace with ourselves. We must devote at least five minutes every day to meditation and resolve to do so even if the world crashes around us. There is nothing else that will give us a helping hand when the whole cosmos is dissolved.

"Come to me, your only refuge. I shall free you from all sins. Have no fear." This assurance that Śri Krishna gives to free us from sin is absolute. So let us learn to be courageous. To tie up an object you wind a string round it again and again. If it is to be untied you will have to do the unwinding in a similar manner. To eradicate the habit of sinning you must develop the habit of doing good to an equal degree. In between there ought to be neither haste nor anger. With haste and anger the thread you keep unwinding will get tangled again. *Īśvara* will come to our help if we have patience, if we have faith in him, and if we are rooted in *dharma*.

The goal of all religions is to wean away man—his mind, his speech, and his body—from sensual pleasure and lead him towards the Lord. Great men have appeared from time to time and established their religions with the goal of releasing people from attachment to their senses, for it is our senses that impel us to sin. "Transitory is the joy derived from sinful action, from sensual pleasure. Bliss is union with the *Paramātman*." Such is the teaching of all religions and their goal is to free man from worldly existence by leading him towards the Lord.

The Purpose of Religion

We know for certain that ordinarily people do not achieve eternal happiness. The purpose of any religion is to lead them towards such happiness. Everlasting blessedness is obtained only by forsaking the quest for petty pleasures. The dictates of *dharma* help us to abandon the pursuit of sensual enjoyments and endeavor

for eternal bliss. They are also essential to create a social order that has the same high purpose, the liberation of all. Religion, with its goal of liberation, lays down the tenets of *dharma*. That is why the great understand the word *dharma* itself to mean religion.

To Be a True Man

The first step in this process of enlightenment is to make a man truly a man, by ensuring that he does not live on an animal level. The second step is to raise him to the heights of divinity. All religions have this goal. They may represent different systems of thought and philosophy. But their concern ought to be that man is not condemned as he is today to a life of desire and anger. All religions speak in one voice that man must be rendered good and that he must be invested with the qualities of love, humility, serenity, and the spirit of sacrifice.

Devotion Common to All Faiths

What is special about *sanātana dharma* (primordial, eternal code of conduct) or Hinduism as it has come to be called? Alone among all religions it reveals the one and only Godhead in many different divine forms, with manifold aspects. The devotee worships the Lord in a form suited to his mental make-up and is thus helped to come closer to the Lord with his love and devotion. These different forms are not the creation of anyone's imagination. The *Paramātman* has revealed himself in these forms to great men and they have had close contact, so to speak, with the deities so revealed. They have also shown us how we too may come face to face with these divinities, given us the *mantras* (Divine formulas) to accomplish this, and also prescribed the manner in which the divine forms, whose vision they have had, are to be adored.

The Kailasanatha Temple at Kanchipuram

Bhakti or devotion is common to all religions whatever the manner of worship they teach. It is not exclusive to our faith in which different deities are reverenced.

The Unity of Religions

All religions have one common ideal: worship of the Lord; and all of them proclaim that there is but one God. This one God accepts your devotion irrespective of the manner of your worship, whether it is according to this or that religion. So there is no need to abandon the religion of your birth and embrace another.

The temple, the church, the mosque, the *vihāra* (a Buddhist monastery; a residence for meditation) may be different from one another. The idol or the symbol in them may not also be the same and the rites performed in them may be different. But the *Paramātman* (Transcendent Unity) who grants grace to the worshipper, whatever be his faith, is the same. The

Jaimuni with the ascetic Mārkandeya Mahāmuni, disciple of Vyāsa

different religions have taken shape according to the customs peculiar to the countries in which they originated and according to the differences in the mental outlook of the people inhabiting them. The goal of all religions is to lead people to the same *Paramātman* according to the different attitudes of the devotees concerned.

One big difference between Hinduism and other faiths is that it does not proclaim that it alone shows the path to liberation. Our Vedic religion alone has not practiced conversion and the reason for it is that our forefathers were well aware that all religions are nothing but different paths to realize the one and only *Paramātman*. The Vedas proclaim: "The wise speak of the One Truth by different names." Śrī Krishna says in the Bhagavad Gītā: "In whatever way or form a man worships me, I increase his faith and make him firm and steady in that worship." This is the reason why Hindus have not practiced—like adherents of other religions—proselytization and religious persecution. Nor have they waged anything like the crusades or *jihāds* (Arabic word for holy war).

All religions that practice conversion employ a certain ritual. For instance, there is baptism in Christianity. Hinduism has more ritual than any other religion, yet its canonical texts do not contain any rite for conversion. No better proof is needed for the fact that we have at no time either encouraged conversion or practiced it.

Śri Chandrasekharendra Saraswati with the present Sankaracharya, Śri Jayendra Saraswati

That the beliefs and customs of the various religions are different cannot be a cause for complaint. Nor is there any need to make all of them similar. The important thing is for the followers of the various faiths to live in harmony with one another. The goal must be unity, not uniformity.

Qualities of Religious Teachers

I believe that the growth or expansion of a religion is in no way related to its doctrines. The common people do not worry about questions of philosophy. A great man of exemplary character and qualities appears on the scene—a great man of compassion who creates serenity everywhere—and people are drawn to him. They become converts to his religion in the firm belief that the doctrines preached by him, whatever they be, must be good. On the other hand, a religion will decline and decay if its spokesmen, however eloquent they are in expounding its concepts, are found to be guilty of lapses in character and conduct. It is difficult to give an answer to the question why people flock to religions that have contradictory beliefs. But, if we examine the history of some religions—how at one time people gloried in them and how these faiths later perished—we shall be able to know the reason. At the same time, it would be possible for us

to find out how in the first place they attracted such a large following. If you find out how a religion declined you will be able to know how it had first grown and prospered.

The decay of a religion in any country could be attributed to the lack of character of its leaders and of the people constituting the establishment responsible for its growth.

We need not be critical of those who indulge in conversion. We need not nurture enmity towards them. What is the reason for them to draw others to their religion by force or temptation? Is it not because of their belief that their religion represents the highest truth? They may engage themselves in conversion in good faith thinking, "Only if our religion is accepted by others, can they have ultimate release. In order to do them such great good, there is nothing wrong in using force or temptations".

If religions that resort neither to force nor to the power of money have grown, it is solely because of the noble qualities of their teachers. Outward guise alone is not what constitutes the qualities of the representative or spokesman of a religion. Whatever the persuasion to which he belongs he must be utterly selfless, bear ill-will towards none, in addition to being morally blameless. He must live an austere life, and must be calm and compassionate by nature. Such a man will be able to help those who come to him by removing their shortcomings and dispelling the evil in them.

Producing men of such noble qualities from amongst us is the way to make our religion flourish. It is not necessary to carry on propaganda against other religions. The need is for representatives, for preceptors, capable of providing an example through their very life of the teachings of our religion. It is through such men that, age after age, *sanātana dharma* has been sustained as a living force. Hereafter too it will be through them that it will continue to remain a living force.

The Vedic Religion: Introductory

The Religion without a Name

We speak of the "Hindu religion", but the religion denoted by the term did not in fact have such a name originally. According to some, the word "Hindu" means "love"; according to some others a Hindu is one who disapproves of *himsā* or violence. This may be an ingenious way of explaining the word.

In none of our ancient *śāstras* (scriptures) does the term "Hindu religion" occur. The name "Hindu" was given us by foreigners. People from the West came to our land across the Sindhu river which they called "*Indus*" or "*Hind*" and the land adjacent to it by the name "India". The religion of this land came to be called "Hindu". The name of a neighboring country is sometimes applied to the land adjacent to it.

Only when there are a number of religions do they have to be identified by different names. But when there is only one, where is the problem of identifying it?

All religions barring our own were established by single individuals. "Buddhism" means the religion founded by Gautama Buddha. Jainism was founded by the Jina called Mahāvīra. So has Christianity its origin in Jesus Christ. Our religion predating all these had spread all over the world. Since there was no other religion to speak about then it was not necessary to give it a name. When I recognized this fact I felt at once that there was no need to be ashamed of the fact that our religion had no name in the past. On the contrary, I felt proud about it.

If ours is a primeval religion, the question arises as to who established it. All inquiries into this question have failed to yield an answer. Was it Vyāsa, who composed the *Brahmasūtra* (one of the great inspired scriptures), the founder of our religion? Or was it Krishna *Paramātman* (Krishna as the incarnation of the Transcendent Unity) who gave us the Bhagavad Gītā? But both Vyāsa and Krishna state that the Vedas existed before them. If that be the case, are we to point to the *risis*, the seers, who gave us the Vedic *mantras*, as the founders of our religion? But they themselves declare: "We did not create the Vedas." When we chant a *mantra* we touch our head with our hand mentioning the name of one seer or another. But the sages themselves say: "It is true that the *mantras* became manifest to the world through us. That is why we are mentioned as the '*mantra risis*'. But the *mantras* were not composed by us but revealed to us. When we sat meditating with our minds under control, the *mantras* were perceived by us in space. Indeed we *saw* them; we did not compose them."

The sacred syllable *Om* in Devanagari

All sounds originate in space. From them arose creation. According to science, the cosmos was produced from the vibrations in space. By virtue of their austerities the sages had the gift of seeing the *mantras* in space, the *mantras* that liberate men from this creation. The Vedas are *apauruṣēya* (not the work of any human author) and are the very breath of the *Paramātman* in his form as space. The sages saw them and made a gift of them to the world.

If we know this truth, we have reason to be proud of the fact that we do not know who founded our religion. In fact we must feel happy that we have the great good fortune to be heirs to a religion that is eternal, a religion containing the Vedas which are the very breath of the *Paramātman*.

Distinctive Features of Sanātana Dharma (Eternal Code of Conduct)

Our religion has a number of unique or distinctive features. One of them is what is called the theory of karma, though this theory is common to religions like Buddhism which are offshoots of Hinduism.

What is the karma doctrine? For every action there is an equal and opposite reaction. There is an ineluctable law of physics governing cause and effect, action and reaction. This law pertaining to physical phenomena our forefathers applied to human life. The cosmos includes not only sentient beings endowed with consciousness but also countless insentient objects. Together they constitute worldly life. The laws, the *dharma*, proper to the first order must apply to the second also. According to the karma theory, every action of a man has an effect corresponding to it. Based on this belief our religion declares that, if a man commits a sin, he shall pay the penalty for it. Also if his act is a virtuous one, he shall reap the benefits thereof.

Our religion further asserts that one is born again and again so as to experience the consequences of one's good and bad actions. "Do good." "Do not do evil," such are the exhortations of all religions. But Hinduism (and its offshoots) alone lay stress on the cause-and-effect connection. No religion originating in countries outside India subscribes to the cause-and-effect connection, nor to the reincarnation theory as one of its articles of faith. Indeed religions originating abroad hold beliefs contrary to this theory and strongly oppose the view that man is born again and again in order to exhaust his karma. They believe that a man has only one birth, that when his soul departs on his death it dwells somewhere awaiting the day of judgment. On this day God makes an assessment of his good and bad actions and, on the basis of it, rewards him with eternal paradise or sentences him to eternal damnation.

That the one and only *Paramātman* who has neither a form nor attributes is manifested as different forms with attributes is another special feature of our religion. We worship idols representing these forms of deities. For this reason others label us polytheists. Their view is utterly wrong. Because we worship the one God, the one Reality, in many different forms it does not mean that we believe in many gods. It is equally absurd to call us idolaters who hold that the idol we worship is God. Hindus with a proper understanding of their religion do not think that the idol alone is God. The idol is meant for the worshipper to offer one-pointed devotion and he adores it with the conviction that the Lord who is present everywhere is present in it also. We see that practitioners of other religions also have symbols for worship and meditation. So it is wholly unjust to believe that Hindus alone worship idols—to regard them with scorn as idolaters is not right.

That ours is the only religion that does not proclaim that its followers have an exclusive right to salvation is a matter of pride for us Hindus. Our catholic outlook is revealed in our scriptures which declare that whatever the religious path followed by people they will fi-

nally attain the same *Paramātman*. That is why there is no place for conversion in Hinduism.

The countries are many and they have different climates and grow different crops. Also each part of the world has evolved a different culture. But the Vedas encompassed lands all over this planet from the very beginning. Later other religions emerged in keeping with the changing attitudes of the nations concerned. That is why aspects of the Vedic tradition are in evidence not only in the religions now in force but in what we know of those preceding them. But in India alone has Hinduism survived as a full-fledged living faith.

It must also be added that this primeval religion has regarded—and still regards—with respect the religions that arose subsequent to it. The Hindu view is this: "Other religions must have evolved according to the degree of maturity of the people among whom they originated. They will bring well-being to their adherents." "Live and let live" has been and continues to be the ideal of our religion. It has given birth to religions like Buddhism and Jainism and they [particularly Buddhism] have been propagated abroad for the Ātmic advancement (progress toward Self-realization) of the people there.

I have spoken about the special characteristics of Hinduism from the philosophical and theological points of view. But it has also another important feature which is also distinctive—the sociological.

All religions have their own philosophical and theological systems. Also all of them deal with individual life and conduct and, to a limited extent, with social life. "Look upon your neighbor as your brother." "Regard your adversary as your friend." "Treat others in the same way as you would like to be treated yourself." "Be kind to all creatures." "Speak the truth." "Practice non-violence." These injunctions and rules of conduct relate to social life up to a point—and only up to a point. To religions other than Hinduism social life or the structure of society is not a major concern. Hinduism alone has a sturdy sociological foundation, and its special feature, *varnāśrama dharma*, is an expression of it.

Varna dharma (caste system) is one concept and *āśrama dharma* (four stages of life) is another—together they make up *varnaśrama dharma*. *Āśrama dharma* deals with the conduct of an individual during different stages of his life. In the first stage, as a *brahmacārin* (student), he devotes himself to studies in a *gurukula* (*āśram*, or home of a guru). In the second stage, as a youth, he takes a wife, settles down in life, and begets children. In the third, as he ages further, he becomes a forest recluse and, without much attachment to worldly life, engages himself in Vedic karma. In the fourth stage, he forsakes even Vedic works, renounces the world utterly to become a *sannyāsin* (ascetic who has renounced the world) and turns his mind towards the *Paramātman*.

These four stages of life or *āśramas* are called *brahmacarya* (student), *garhasthya* (householder), *vānaprastha* (forest dweller) and *sannyāsa* (ascetic).

Varna dharma (caste) is an "arrangement" governing all society. It is very much a target of attack today and is usually spoken of as the division of society into *jātis* (sub-divisions of the castes). But *varna* and *jāti* are in fact different. There are only four *varnas* but the *jātis* are numerous.

Critics of *varna dharma* brand it as "a blot on our religion" and as "a vicious system which divides people into high and low". But, if you look at it impartially, you will realize that it is a unique instrument to bring about orderly and harmonious social life.

The Vedas, the Root of All

We find that there is but one scripture as the source common to the different sects and schools of thought in the Hindu religion.

This source includes the Upanishads. The great teachers of the Śiva, Vishnu, and Śankara traditions have written commentaries on ten of the Upanishads. The Upanishadic texts proclaim that the *Brahman* is the one and only Godhead. In one Upanishad It is called Vishnu;[1] in another It is called Śiva.[2] All the deities mentioned in the Vedas—Mitra, Varuna, Agni, Indra and so on—are different names of the same Truth. So it is said in the Vedas: "*Ekam sath viprā bahudhā vadanti.*" (It is the one truth, which *jnānins* call by different names.)

It emerges that for all the divisions in our religion there is but one scripture—a scripture common to all—and one Godhead which is known by many names. The Vedas are the common scripture and the Godhead common to all is the *Brahman*. Thus we can say with finality, and without any room for doubt, that all of us belong to the same religion.

The Vedas that constitute the scripture common to all and which reveal the Godhead that is common to us also teach us how to lead our life, and—this is important—they do us the ultimate good by showing us in the end the way to become that very Godhead ourselves. They are our refuge both here and in the hereafter and are the source and root of all our different traditions, all our systems of thought. All sects, all schools of our religion, have their origin in them. The root is one but the branches are many.

The Vedas are the source not only of the various divisions of Hinduism, all the religions of the world may be traced back to them. It is our bounden duty to preserve them for all time to come with their glory undiminished.

The Vedas in their Original Form

Some do not seem to attach any special significance to the fact that the Vedas are in Sanskrit. They think that these sacred texts could be known through translations.

Nowadays a number of books are translated from one language into another and in this process the original form or character is changed or distorted. The words spoken by a great man on a particular subject may not be fully understood today. But if they are preserved in the original in the same language, there is the possibility of their meaning being fully grasped at some future date. You use a beautiful word to convey an idea in your language, but its equivalent may not be found in any other tongue. Also, it may become necessary to express the same in a roundabout way.

There is also the possibility that the opinion expressed first, in its original context, may not come through effectively in a translation. We must consider the further disadvantage of the translation being circumscribed by the mental make-up of the translator, the limitations of his knowledge and understanding of the subject dealt with. The translation done by one may not seem right to another. When there are a number of translations of the same work, it would be hard to choose the right one. We shall then be compelled to go back to the original.

This is the reason why I insist that the Vedas must be preserved in their original form. They are the source of the philosophical systems associated with the great *ācāryas* (teachers). These masters evolved their doctrines without making any modifications in the Vedas to suit themselves; nor did they establish any religions of their own outside the Vedic tradition. The source, the root, of their systems of thought is one and the same—the Vedas. It is because this source has remained unchanged in its original character that thinkers and teachers have, from time to time, been able to draw inspiration and strength from it to present new viewpoints. But these viewpoints have not meant the creation of new religions. The reason is that all of them—all these systems—belong to the larger system called the Vedic religion.

Homam (ritual Vedic sacrifice) in progress at Kumbakonam Sankara Mutt

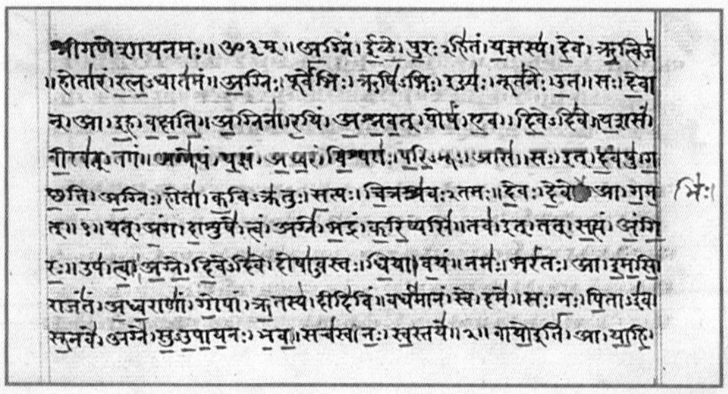

Page from the *Rigveda*

Veda *parayanam* (reading religious texts)

The Vedic Religion and Varna (Caste) Dharma

What is Varna (Caste) Dharma?

In other countries other physicians have prescribed medicines in the form of their own religious systems. Would your doctor like to be told that he should treat you in the same way as another doctor treats his patient? There are several systems of medicine. In one there is a strict diet regimen, in another there is not much strictness about the patient's food. In one system the medicines administered taste sweet; in another they taste bitter. To be restored to health we have to follow strictly any one method of treatment, not insist on a combination of the various therapies.

Other religions lay down only such duties as are common to all their followers. In the Vedic religion there are two types of *dharma*, the one being common to all and the other to individual *varnas* (castes). The duties common to all Hindus, the universal code of conduct, have the name of *sāmānya dharma*. Non-violence, truthfulness, cleanliness, control of the senses, non-acquisitiveness (one must not possess material goods in excess of what is needed for one's bare requirements, not even a straw must one own in excess), devotion to *Īśvara*, trust in one's parents, love for all creatures—these form part of the *sāmānya dharma*. Then each *varna* has its own special code of conduct or *viśēsha dharma* determined by its hereditary vocation.

It is difficult to say how long people will continue to owe allegiance to the religions that arose in various countries during historical times. I say this not because I happen to be a representative of Hindus nor is it my wish to speak in demeaning terms about other religions. My wish is indeed that people following different religions ought to continue to remain in their respective folds and find spiritual fulfillment in them. I do not invite others to embrace my faith. In fact I believe that to do so is contrary to the basic tenets of my religion. Nothing occurs in this world as an accident. People with different levels of maturity are born in different religions: so it is ordained by the Lord. I believe that a man grows inwardly by practicing the tenets of the religion of his birth.

If I speak about what I feel to be the worthy features of Hinduism—features that are not found in other religions—it is neither to speak ill of the latter nor to invite their followers to our side. Non-Hindus attack these unique aspects of our religion without taking the trouble of understanding them and some Hindus themselves are influenced by their views. That is why I am constrained to speak about the distinctive doctrines of our religion. Acceptance of concepts like karma, the Lord's incarnations, etc, will in no way weaken their [non-Hindus'] attachment to the basic beliefs of their own religions. What is the fundamental concept of any religion, its living principle? It is faith in the Lord and devotion to him. For others to view these special concepts of Hinduism sympathetically does not mean that their faith in God or devotion to him will be affected in any way.

I say all this not because I think that other religions are in any trouble, nor because I have reason to be happy if indeed they are. I merely repeat the view that lack of faith in religion—indeed atheism—is growing day by day everywhere and that all religions are struggling for their survival.

Divided by Work but Still of One Heart

Any society has to depend on the proper execution of a variety of jobs. It is from this social necessity that the concept of division of labor arose. But who is to decide the number of people for each type of work? Who is to determine the proportions for society to function in a balanced manner? In the West they had no answer to these questions. Everybody there competes with everybody else for comfortable jobs and everywhere you find greed and bitterness resulting from such rivalries. And, as a consequence of all this, there are lapses from discipline and morality.

In our country we based the division of labor on a hereditary system and, while it worked, people had a happy, peaceful, and contented life. Today even a multimillionaire is neither contented nor happy. Then even a cobbler led a life without cares. What sort of progress have we achieved today by inflaming evil desires in all hearts and pushing everyone into the slough of discontent? Not satisfied with such "progress" there is talk everywhere that we must go forward rapidly in this manner.

Greed and covetousness were unknown during the centuries when *varna dharma* flourished. People were bound together in small well-knit groups and they discovered that there was happiness in their being together. Besides they had faith in religion, fear of God and devotion, and a feeling of pride in their own family deities and in the modes of worshipping them. In this way they found fullness in their lives without any need to suffer the hunger and disquiet of seeking external objects. All society experienced a sense of well-being.

One more point must be considered. Even if you concede that the social divisions have caused bitterness among the different sections here, what about the same in other countries? Can the existence of such ill-will in other lands be denied? The differences there, based on wealth and status, cause bitterness and resentment among the underprivileged and poorer sections. In America, it is claimed that all people have enough food, clothing, and housing. They say that even a domestic servant there owns a car. It is reasonable to infer from this that the Americans are a contented people. But what is the reality there? The man who has only one car is envious of another who has two. Similarly, the fact that one person has a bank balance of a hundred million dollars is cause for heart-burning for another with a bank balance of only a million. Those who have sufficient means to live comfortably quarrel with people better off over rights and privileges. Does this not mean that even in a country like the United States there are conflicts between the higher and lower classes of society?

It seems to me that better than the distinctions prevailing in the West—distinctions that give rise to jealousies and social discord—are the differences mistakenly attributed to the hereditary system of vocations. In the old days this arrangement ensured peace in the land with everyone living a contented life. There was neither envy nor hatred and everyone readily accepted his lot.

The different types of work are meant for the good of the people in general. It is wrong to believe that one job belongs to an "inferior"

category and another to a "superior" type. There is no more efficacious medicine for inner purity than doing one's work, whatever it be, without any desire for reward and doing it to perfection. I must add that even wrong notions about work (one job being better than another or worse) is better than the disparities and differences to be met with in other countries. We are [or were] free from the spirit of rivalry and bitterness that vitiate social life there.

Divided we have remained united, and nurtured our civilization. Other civilizations have gone under because the people of the countries concerned, though seemingly united, were in fact divided. In our case, though there were differences in the matter of work, there was unity of hearts and that is how our culture and civilization flourished. In other countries the fact that there were no distinctions based on vocations (anyone could do any work) itself gave rise to rivalries and eventually to disunity. They were not able to withstand the onslaught of other civilizations.

It is not practicable to make all people one, nor can everyone occupy the same high position. At the same time it is also unwise to keep people divided into classes that are like water-tight compartments.

The *Dharmaśāstras* (scriptures on *dharma*) have shown us a middle way that avoids the pitfalls of the two extremes. I have come as a representative of this way and that is why I speak for it: that there ought to be distinctions among various sections of people in the performance of rites but that there must be unity of hearts. There should be no confusion between the two.

Though we are divided outwardly in the matter of work, with unity of hearts there will be peace. That was the tradition for ages together in this land—there was oneness of hearts. If every member of society does his duty, does his work, unselfishly and with the conviction that he is doing it for the good of all, considerations of high and low will not enter his mind. If people carry out the duties common to them, however adverse the circumstances be, and if every individual performs the duties that are special to him, no one will have cause for suffering at any time.

Why Only in This Country?

How did we lose our inner vitality? By giving up our traditions we have become weak. What was it that nurtured our civilization and kept it growing for thousands of years? By parting with our traditions we descended so low as to be ashamed of calling ourselves heirs to this civilization. The fact is that, so long as we practiced *varna dharma* (caste system), which is unique to our country, our civilization stood like a rock arousing the admiration of all the world. But after this *dharma* began to decline we have been on the descent day by day.

Why should this country alone practice *varna dharma*? Because this *dharma* is necessary if we want to sustain a civilization that can promote the growth of philosophy, nourish our arts and culture, inspire us more and more in our inward search and help us in the realization of the Godhead. If the *varna* system is followed at least in this country, it will be an example to the rest of the world.

If there is no *varna dharma*, it means at once the growth of social disharmony, the rise of jealousies, and discontent among the people. Men will compete with one another for the jobs they like or are convenient to them. There will be competition for education on the same lines. Since all will not succeed in their efforts or in their desire or ambition being satisfied, the result will be hatred and resentment everywhere.

No civilization can flourish in the absence of a system that brings fulfillment to all. *Varna dharma* brought fulfillment and satisfaction to all.

The Varadaraja Perumal Temple Tank at Kanchipuram

The Conflict between Tradition and Modernity

Politicians and intellectuals alike say that *varna* (caste) is part of an uncivilized system. Why? Who is responsible for the disintegration of so worthy an arrangement as *varna dharma*?

These are questions that I raised earlier and I shall try to answer them. The wrong ideas that have developed about *varna dharma* must be ascribed to the Brahmins themselves. They are indeed responsible for the decay of an ages-old system that contributed not only to our Ātmic advancement (progress toward Self-realization) but also to the well-being of the nation as well as of all mankind.

The Brahmin relinquished the duties of his birth—the study of the Vedas and performance of the rites laid down in the Vedic tradition. He left his birthplace, the village, for the town. He cropped his hair and started dressing in European style. Giving up the Vedas, he took to the mundane learning of the West. He fell to the lure of jobs offered by his white master and aped him in dress, manners, and attitudes. He threw to the winds the noble *dharma* he had inherited from the Vedic seers through his forefathers and abandoned all for a mess of pottage. He was drawn to everything Western, science, life-style, entertainment.

The canonical texts have it that the Brahmin must have no love for money, that he must not accumulate wealth. So long as he followed his *dharma*, as prescribed by the *śāstras*, and so long as he chanted the Vedas and performed sacrifices, he brought good to the world, and all other castes respected him and treated him with affection.

Others now observed how the Brahmin had changed, how his life-style had become different with all its glitter and show and how he went about with all the pretence of having risen on the scale of civilization. The Brahmin had been an ideal for them in all that is noble, but now he strayed from the path of *dharma*; and following his example they too gave up their traditional vocations that had brought them happiness and contentment and left their native village to settle in towns. Like the Brahmin they became keen to learn English and secure jobs in the government.

A question that arises in this context is how Vedic studies which had not suffered much even during Muslim rule received a severe setback with the advent of the European. One reason is the impact of the new sciences and the machines that came with the white man. Granted that many a truth was revealed through these sciences—and this was all to the good up to a point. But we must remember that the knowledge of a subject per se is one thing and how we use it in practice is another.

The introduction of steam power and electricity made many types of work easier but it also meant comforts hitherto unthought-of to gratify the senses. If you keep pandering to the senses more and more new desires are engendered. This will mean the production of an increasing number of objects of pleasure. The more we try to obtain sensual pleasure the more we will cause injury to our innermost being. The new pleasures that could be had with scientific development and the introduction of machines were an irresistible lure for the Brahmin as they were to other communities. Another undesirable product of the sciences brought by the white man was rationalism which undermined people's faith in religion and persuaded some to believe that the religious truths that are based on faith and are inwardly experienced are nothing but deception. The man who did not give up his duties even during Muslim rule now abandoned them for the new-found pleasures and comforts. He dressed more smartly than the Englishman, smoked cigarettes, and even learned to dance like his white master. Those who thus became proficient in the arts of the white man were rewarded with jobs.

Now occurred the biggest tragedy.

Up till now all members of society had their hereditary jobs to do and they did not have to worry about their livelihood. Now, with the example of the Brahmin before them, members of other castes also gave up their traditional occupations for the jobs made available by the British in the banks, railways, collectorates, etc. With the introduction of machinery our handicrafts fell into decay and many of our artisans had to look for other means of livelihood. In the absence of any demarcation in the matter of work and workers, there arose competition for jobs for the first time in the country. It was a disastrous development and it generated jealousy, ill-will, disputes, and a host of other evils among people who had hitherto lived in harmony.

Ill feelings developed between Brahmins and non-Brahmins also. How? Brahmins formed only a small percentage of the population. But they were able to occupy top positions in the new order owing to their intelligence which was the result of the spiritual efforts of their forefathers. They excelled in all walks of life—in administration, in academics, in law, in medicine, engineering, and so on. The white man made his own calculations about developing animosity between Brahmins and non-Brahmins and realized that by fuelling it he could strengthen his hold on the country. He fabricated the Aryan-Dravidian theory of races and the seeds of differences were sown among children born of the same mother. It was a design that proved effective in a climate already made unhealthy by rivalry for jobs.

The Brahmin spoiled himself and spoiled others. By abandoning his *dharma* he be-

came a bad example to others. Now, after he had divested himself of his *dharma*, there was nothing to give him distinction, to mark him out from others. As a matter of fact, even by strictly adhering to his *dharma* the Brahmin is not entitled to feel superior to others. He must always remain humble in the belief that "everyone performs a function in society; I perform mine". If at all, others respected him in the past and accorded him a high place in society, it was in consideration of his selfless work, his life of austerity, discipline, and purity. Now he had descended to such depths as to merit their most abrasive criticism.

Is it not better then to starve and yet be attached firmly to our *dharma* so long as there is breath in us? Is not such loyalty to our *dharma* a matter of pride? Why should we care about how others see us, whether they honor us or speak ill of us? So long as we do not compete with them for jobs they will have no cause for jealousy or resentment. Let them call us backward or stupid or think that we are not capable of keeping abreast of the times. Are we not now already their butt of ridicule? Let us be true to our *dharma* in the face of the mockery of others, even in the face of death. Is not such a lot preferable to suffering the slings of scorn and criticism earned by forsaking our *dharma* for the sake of filling our belly? People nowadays die for their motherland; they lay down their lives for their mother tongue. Was there any demonstration of faith like this, such willingness to die for a cause or a belief, when the British came here with their life-style? At that time did we protect our *dharma* with courage, in the belief that even death was a small price to pay for it?

The Lord himself has declared in the Gītā that it is better to die abiding by one's *dharma* than prosper through another man's *dharma*. Brahmins who had seen no reason to change their life-style during the long Muslim period of our history changed it during British rule. Why? New sciences and machinery came with the white man. The motor car and electricity had their own impact on life here. Brahmins were drawn to comforts and conveniences not thought of before. This could be a reason for their change of life, but not a justification.

The Brahmin is not to regard his body as a means for the enjoyment of sensual pleasures but as an instrument for the observance of such rites as are necessary to protect the Vedas—and the Vedas have to be protected for the welfare of mankind. The basic *dharma* is that to the body of the Brahmin nothing must be added that incites his sensual appetite. It was a fundamental mistake on the part of the Brahmin to have forgotten the spirit of sacrifice that imbues his *dharma* and become a victim of the pleasures and comforts easily obtained from the new gadgets and instruments. There is pride in adhering to one's *dharma* even when one is faced with adverse circumstances. Brahmins (during British rule) committed a grave mistake by not doing so and we are suffering the consequences. See the ill-will in the country today among children of the same mother. We have created suffering for others also. At first Brahmins were denied admission to colleges and refused jobs. Now things have come to such a pass that other communities also suffer the same fate.

All was well so long as man, using his own innate resources, lived a simple life without the help of machines. With more and more factories and increasing machine power, life itself has become complicated. The situation today is such that everyone is facing difficulties in getting admission to college or in getting a job.

People ask me: "What is the remedy today? Do you expect all Brahmins to leave their new life-style and return to Vedic learning?" Whether or not I expect them to do so and whether or not such a step seems possible, I must ask them to do so (to return to their Vedic *dharma*). Where is the need for a *guru-pītha* (*āśram*) or a seat on which an *ācārya* (great teacher) is installed if I am to keep my mouth shut and watch idly as the *dharma* that is the source of everything is being endangered? Even if it seems not possible (Brahmins returning to the *dharma* of their birth) it must be shown to be possible in practice: that is the purpose of the *āśrams*. They must harness all their energies towards the attainment of this goal.

The Least Expected of Brahmins

This is the least Brahmins can do to preserve the Vedic traditions. Arrangements to impart Vedic learning to children must be made in every Brahmin household. I know that there are not enough teachers, a sad reflection on the state of our *dharma*. Considering this and the likely economic condition of parents I would suggest that Veda classes may be conducted for all children together of a locality or neighborhood. Children of poor families may be taught on a cooperative basis.

Veda *patashala* students at Vishnu Kanchi

Step by step in this way the boys will be able to memorize the *mantra* part of the Vedas and also learn how to conduct rites like *upākarma* (first step for a young boy to become a Vedic student). I speak here about *prayoga*, the conduct or procedure of rites, because in the absence of priests in the future everyone should be able to perform Vedic rites himself.

Young Brahmins in the temple at Madurai

The sound of the Vedas must pervade the world for all time to come. Everyone must sincerely work towards achieving this end. It is your duty to ensure the good not only of the Brahmin community, not only of all the castes of India, but of all the countless creatures of earth. It is a duty imposed on you by *Īśvara*—it is a divine duty.

It is important that we perform this duty we owe to the people of the present. But it is equally important that we perform it so as to be saved from committing a crime against future generations. "As it is nobody cares for the Vedas," you are likely to tell me. "Who is going to care for them in the coming years? What purpose is served by all the efforts we take now to keep up their study?" I do not share this view. When the wheel keeps turning, that part of it which is now down has necessarily to come up. Modern civilization with its frenzied pace is bound to have its fall after attaining its peak. We have been carried away by the supposed comforts made possible by advanced technology. But one day we will realize that they do not give us any feeling of fullness and that we have indeed created only discomforts for ourselves through them.

Preserving the Vedas: Why it Is a Lifetime Mission

"The sages transcended the frontiers of human knowledge and became one with the Universal Reality. It is through them that the world received the Vedic *mantras*," this is one of the basic concepts of our religion. If you do not accept that human beings can obtain such Ātmic Power as exemplified by these seers, any further talk on the subject would be futile. One could point out to you great men whom you can see for yourself, great men who have perfected themselves and acquired powers not shared by the common people. But if you think of them to be cheats or fraudulent men, any further talk would again be useless. In our present state of limited understanding, the argument that denies the existence of anything beyond the range of human reason and comprehension itself betrays the height of irrationalism.

Are sounds and vibrations spontaneously produced? No. If vibrations arise on their own they will be erratic and confusing and not related to one another. But what do we see in the cosmos? There is a certain orderliness about it and one thing in it is linked to another. What do we infer from this? That a Great Intelligence has formulated this scheme that we see, that it has created it from its own vibrations.

The Vedas are sounds emanating from the vibrations of this Great Intelligence, the Great

A Vedic teacher with *sishyas* (pupils) in Rameswaram

His Holiness Śri Jayendra Saraswati with young Brahmins

Gnosis. That is why we believe that the *mantras* of the Vedas originate from the *Paramātman* himself. We must take special care of such sounds to ensure the good of the world. Yes, the Vedic *mantras* are sequences of sounds that are meant for the good of the world.

Whatever is present in space is also present in the individual being. These elements exist in the human body in a form that is accessible to the senses. The sounds a person makes in his throat have their source in space in a form not audible to us. The radio transforms electrical waves into sound waves. If a man can grasp the sounds in space and make them audible, he will be able to create with them what is needed for the good of the world. Yoga is the science that accomplishes such a task. Through yogic practice (perfection) one can become aware of what is in the macrocosm and draw it into the microcosm. I shall not be able to give you proof of this in a form acceptable to human reason. Yoga transcends our limited reason and understanding. The purpose of the Vedas is to speak about matters that are beyond the comprehension of the human mind.

You must have faith in the words of great men or else, to know the truth of such matters, you must practice yoga strictly observing its rules. It may not be practicable for all those who ask questions or harbor doubts about the Vedas to practice yoga in this manner. Even if you are prepared to accept the words of a true yogin, how are you, in the first place, to be convinced that he is indeed a true yogin and not a fraud? Altogether it means that you must have faith in someone, in something. Later such faith will be strengthened from your own observations, inference, and experience. There is no point in speaking to people who have either no faith or refuse to develop it through their own experience.

There is a state in which the macrocosm and the microcosm are perceived as one. Great men there are who have reached such a state and are capable of transforming what is subtle in the one into what is gross in the other. I am speaking here to those who believe in such a possibility.

When we look at this universe and the complex manner in which it functions, we realize that there must be a Great Wisdom that has created it and sustains it. It is from this Great Wisdom, that is the *Paramātman*, that all that we see are born and it is from It that all the sounds that we hear have emanated. First came the universe of sound and then the universe that we observe. Most of the former still exists in space. All that exists in the outer universe is present in the human body also. The space that exists outside us exists also in our heart.

The *mantras* of the Vedas are remarkable in that they bring blessings to the world in the form of sound—even if their meaning is not understood. Of course, they are pregnant with meaning and represent the lofty principle that it is the One Truth that is manifested as all that we perceive. They also confer blessings on us by taking the form of deities appropriate to the different sounds (of the *mantras*).

Sound does not bring any benefits, any fruits, by itself. *Īśvara* alone is the bestower of benefits. However, instead of making the fruits available to us directly, he appoints deities to distribute them in the same manner as the king or president of a country appoints officials to carry out his dictates. The *mantras* represent various deities in the form of sound. If we attain perfection (*siddhi*) by constant chanting and meditation of a *mantra*, it should be possible for us to see the deity invoked in his physical form. The deities also arise if we make offerings into the sacrificial fire reciting specific *mantras*. If a sacrifice is conducted in this manner, the deities give us their special blessings. We do not pay taxes directly to the king or president. In the same way, we pay taxes in the form of sacrifices and Vedic chanting to the aides of the *Paramātman* for the sake of the welfare of the world. The sounds of the *mantras* constitute their form.

The Vedas have won the admiration of Western scholars for their poetic beauty. They bring us face to face with many deities—they bring us also their grace. Above all, through

Deity at the wall shrine of Kailasanatha temple at Kanchipuram

the Upanishads they teach us the great truths relating to the Self. The Vedas are thus known for the profundity of the truths contained in them, but their sound is no less important. Indeed their sound has its own significance and power. All *mantras*, it must be noted, have power, not only Vedic *mantras*.

The Vedic *mantras* do good to all creatures in this world and the hereafter: we must have implicit faith in this belief. It is not proper to ask whether what we ourselves cannot hear with our ears will be heard by the seers. There is such a thing as the divine power of seeing and hearing. Our sight is dependent on the lens in our eyes. Were this lens different what we observe would also be different. Through the intense practice of yoga we can obtain the divine power of seeing and hearing.

We must not inquire into the Vedas with our limited powers of perception and with our limited capacity to reason and comprehend. The Vedas speak to us about what is beyond the reach of our eyes and ears and reasoning—that is their very purpose. There are things that we comprehend through direct perception. We do not need the help of the Vedas to know about them. What cannot be proved by reasoning and what is beyond the reach of our intellect—these seers have gifted us in the form of the Vedas with their divine perception.

The question that now occurs is why there should be a separate caste committed to Vedic learning and Vedic practices even if it is conceded that Vedic *mantras* have the power to do good.

In answering this question we must first remember that the Vedas are not to be read from the written text. They have to be memorized by constant listening and repeated chanting. The learner then becomes a teacher himself and in this manner the process goes on from generation to generation. Maintaining such a tradition of learning and teaching is a whole-time occupation. Neither the teacher nor the taught may take up any other work.

We must also remember that the Brahmin is expected to master subjects other than the Vedas also, like the arts and crafts and the various sciences. He has in fact to learn the vocations of other *jātis* (sub-divisions of castes)—but he must not take up any for his own livelihood. It is the responsibility of the Brahmin to promote knowledge and culture. He is expected to learn the hereditary skills of all *jātis*, including the art of warfare, and pass on these skills to the respective *jātis* to help them earn their livelihood. The Brahmin's calling is learning and teaching the Vedas. According to the *śāstras* he must live in a modest dwelling, observe strict rules and vows so as to gain mastery of the *mantras*. He must eat only as much as is needed to keep body and soul together. All temptations to make money and enjoy sensual pleasures he must sternly resist. All his actions must be inspired by the spirit of sacrifice and he must pass his days sustaining the Vedic tradition and practices for the good of mankind.

It is the duty of other *varnas* (castes) to see that the Brahmin does not die of starvation. They must provide him with the bare necessities of life and such materials as are needed for the performance of sacrifices. Wages are paid to those who do other jobs or a price is paid for what they produce. The Brahmin works for the whole community and serves it by chanting *mantras*, by performing sacrifices, and by leading a life according to the dictates of religion. That is why he must be provided with his upkeep. The canonical texts do not say that we must build him a palace or that he must be given gifts of gold. The Brahmin must be provided with the wherewithal for the proper performance of sacrifices. In his personal life he must eschew all show and luxury. It is by taming his senses—by burning away all desire—that he gains mastery over the *mantras*.

All mankind, all creatures of earth, must live in happiness. Everybody must practice his allotted *dharma* for the good of all with the realization that there is no question of any work being "higher" than any other or "lower". Preserving the sound of the Vedas must remain the duty of one class so as to ensure plenty in this world as well as to create universal Ātmic uplift. To revert to the question I put to you first. Leaving aside the vocation of the Vedic

Initiation into Vedic instruction or sacred knowledge

Donning the sacred thread

dharma, let us assume that the hereditary system is beneficial in respect of all types of work. But why should the preservation of the Vedic *dharma* be the lifelong vocation of one class? It is now established, as I conclude, that however it may be with the other vocations, whether or not they exist, whether or not there is a mix-up in them, the pursuit of the Vedic *dharma* must remain a separate calling.

Our society must be one in which there are no differences of high and low. All will then live in harmony as the children of *Īśvara* without fighting among themselves. They will live as a united family helping one another and spreading a sense of peace and happiness everywhere.

My Work

It does not matter if you are unable to create conditions in which Brahmins henceforth will make the pursuit of the Vedic *dharma* their lifelong vocation. All I ask you is the minimum you can do: make arrangements to impart to your children the Vedic *mantras*, to teach them the scripture for at least one hour a day from the time they are eight years old until they are eighteen. Teach them also the *prayoga* (the conduct of rites). Do this on a cooperative basis in each locality. If you succeed in this you will have truly honored me with a shower of gold coins.

It gives me joy that more and more *bhajans* (sacred singing ceremonies) are conducted in the towns than before, that work connected with temples is on the increase, and that purānic discourses (discourses on traditional stories) are given more often than before. But we must remember that the Vedas constitute the basis of all these. If our scripture suffers a decline, how long will the activities based on it survive? The Vedas must be handed down from father to son, from one generation to the next. It is because we have forgotten this tradition that our religion itself has become shaky. All the trouble in the world, all the suffering and all the evil must be attributed to the fact that the Brahmin has forsaken his *dharma*, the Vedic *dharma*.

I am not worried about the system of *varnas* being destroyed, but I am worried about the setback to the welfare of mankind. I am also extremely concerned about the fact that, if the Vedic tradition which has been maintained like a chain from generation to generation is broken, it may not be possible to create the tradition all over again.

The good arising in a subtle form from the sound of the Vedas and the performance of sacrifices is not the only benefit that constitutes the welfare of mankind. From *Vedānta* are derived lofty truths that can bring Ātmic uplift to people belonging to all countries. How did foreigners come to have an interest in our *Vedānta*? When they came to India they discovered here a class of people engaged in the practice of the Vedic *dharma* as a lifetime calling. They were curious to find out in what way the Vedas were great that an entire class of people should have dedicated themselves to them all their life. They conducted research into these scriptures and discovered many truths including those pointing to the unity of the various cultures of the world.

His Holiness Śri Jayendra Saraswati at the *homam* venue

The Kailasanatha Temple at Kanchipuram

The Śāstras (Scriptures) and Modern Life

The Cure for the Disease Called Modern Civilization

It is important to realize that if we are to remain true to the *śāstras* it is not because they represent the views of the seers but because they contain the rules founded on the Vedas which are nothing but what *Īśvara* has ordained. That is the reason why we must follow them. It is my duty to see that the *śāstras* are preserved as they are. I have no authority to change them.

We must not give up the śāstric way of life thinking it to be difficult to follow. If we are not carried away by the glitter of modern mundane life, if we reduce our wants and do not run after money, there will be no need to abandon the customs and rites laid down by our canonical texts. If we are not obsessed with making money there will be plenty of time to think of the Lord. And peace, contentment, and happiness will reign.

Money is not essential to the performance of the rites enjoined by the *śāstras*, nor is pomp and circumstance essential to worship. Even dried *tulasī* and *bilvā* leaves are enough to perform *pūjā* (daily offering rites). "Marriage also is a śāstric ceremony. We spend a lot of money on it. What about such expenses?" it is asked. All the lavish display we see at weddings today are unnecessary and do not have the sanction of the scriptures. Specifically, the dowry that forms such a substantial part of the marriage expenses has no scriptural sanction at all. If money were important to the performance of the rites enjoined by our canonical texts it would mean that our religion is meant for rich people. In truth it is not so.

Of the four goals of life—*dharma*, material acquisitions, desire, and liberation—we seek gratification of *kāma* (desire) alone in the form of pleasure, love, etc. And to have our desires satisfied we keep struggling to acquire material things. Our efforts must be directed towards obtaining liberation through the practice of *dharma*. All that we need to do for this ideal is to resolve to live a simple life. There should then be no compulsion to run after money and other material goods. It would naturally become easier for us to practice *dharma* and reap the ultimate fruit—that is eternal bliss.

Religion and Society

If our goal were but a comfortable and happy life in this world, matters concerning social life could be changed now and again. But ours is an exalted goal and it concerns the Self. The rules of worldly life are in keeping with this high purpose and they cannot be changed according to our convenience. The *śāstras* (scriptures) do not regard happiness in this world as of paramount importance. They teach us how we may experience joy in the other world even by suffering many kinds of hardships or discomforts here. So it is not right to seek changes in them to suit our worldly existence.

The views of the reformers must have been shaped by our present system of education and so it is no use blaming them. In other countries no contradiction exists between their religion and their system of education. Unfortunately, the schools established by the British in India had nothing to do with our religion. People were compelled to take to Western education for the sake of their livelihood. Soon a situation arose in which they came to be steeped from childhood itself in an alien system of instruction. They had therefore no way of developing acquaintance with, or faith in, our ancient *śāstras*. And, since they were kept ignorant of their scriptures and their underlying purpose, they persuaded themselves to take the view that the *śāstras* could be changed according to their convenience.

Our youngsters are exposed to criticism of our religion and our sacred texts from a tender age. They are told that the *Purāṇās* (traditional stories) are a tissue of lies, that the *śāstras* help the growth of superstition. How can they have any attachment to our faith, to its rites, and traditions?

Faith in religion and God must be inculcated in people from their childhood. They must get to know about great men who lived and continue to live an exemplary life true to the tenets of our religion. Faith in the works of the seers must be instilled in them, works based on the experience of the seers themselves, experience beyond a life of sensation, and pointing the way to spiritual uplift. They must also be helped to believe that the *ṛṣis* (seers) formulated the *śāstras* in such a way as to make worldly happiness and social life subservient to the advancement of the Self. Only then will people recognize that the rules of religion have a far higher purpose than the comforts and conveniences of temporal life.

Neither too much Ease nor too many Comforts

In this century, people seek ostentatious living in the name of progress. So long as the hunger for new comforts continues, neither the individual nor society will have contentment and there will always be feelings of rivalry, jealousy, and heart-burning among people. In the *varnaśrama dharma*, the Brahmin and non-Brahmin are equal economically speaking. In spite of the caste differences, the same simple living is enjoined on all. The ideal of equality can be achieved only if all people live a simple life. In this order every individual experiences contentment and inner happiness and no one has cause of envying others their prosperity.

No man, whatever his vocation, should have either too much money or too many comforts. Above all what is important is that for which all these are intended but that which cannot be truly obtained through them: contentment and a sense of fullness within. Only when there is inner satisfaction can one meditate on the Lord. And only in the mind of a man who has such contentment is the Ultimate Truth realized as a reality. When a person has too many comforts he will be incapable of going beyond the stage of sensual pleasures. If he is addicted to enjoyments, without any need for physical exertion, he will do injury to his mind, and his inner being. Hard work and the capacity to suffer discomforts are essential for those who yearn for Ātmic uplift. They will then learn to realize that there is comfort in discomfort and in hard work.

Śāstra or Conscience?

In matters of the Self, of *dharma* and religion, the Vedas are in the forefront as our guide. Next come the *Dharmaśāstras* (inspired scriptures on *dharma*). Third is the conduct of the great sages of the past. Fourth is the example of the virtuous people of our own times. Conscience comes last in determining *dharma*.

Now everything has become topsy-turvy. People give importance first to their conscience and last to the Vedas. We must consult our conscience only as a last resort when we have no other means of knowing what is *dharma* with reference to our actions. Conscience is fit to be only a witness (*sākṣī*), not to be a judge. A witness often gives false evidence. The mind, however, does not tell an untruth—indeed it knows the truth of all things. "There is no deceit that is hidden from the heart (mind)," says Avvai. Conscience may be regarded as a witness. But nowadays it is brought in as a judge also in dhārmic matters. As a witness it will give us a true report of what it sees or has seen. But on the basis of it we cannot give a decision on what is just with any degree of finality. "What I think is right": everybody would try to satisfy himself thus about his actions if he were to be guided only by his conscience. How can this be justified as the verdict of *dharma*?

We often hear people say, "I will act according to what my conscience tells me." This is not a right attitude. All at once your conscience cannot be given the place of a judge. It is only when there is no other way open to you that you may tell your mind: "You have seen everything as a witness. Now tell me your opinion." The mind belongs to each one of us as individuals. So it cannot be detached from our selfish interests. The place it has in one's personal affairs cannot be given to it in matters of religion. On questions of *dharma* the opinion of sages alone is valid, sages who were concerned with universal welfare and who transcended the state of the individual concerned with his own mind, or with himself.

The Vedas

The Basic Texts of Hinduism: Our Ignorance of Them

Our religious texts must be taught early in life. When a child grows up and goes to college, he believes his studies will perhaps prove useful to him. If he reads for a B.L. or LL.B. degree, it is to become a lawyer. Similarly, if he reads for an L.T. (or B.Ed.) degree or an M.B.B.S., it is to become a teacher or a doctor. If you ask a teenager to study our religious texts, he would retort: "Why should I learn them? How will it help me in my career?" So religious texts should be taught in childhood, that is, before the youngster is old enough to question you about their utility or harbor doubts about the texts. Only then will he develop an interest in our religion and *śāstras*. Do we pay our children for their being interested in sports, music, or cinema? Similarly, they must be made to take an interest in religion also and such interest must be created in the same way as in sports and entertainment. If children take to sports and entertainment which afford only temporary pleasure, they are bound to take to religion which will confer on them everlasting happiness. The present sorry state of affairs is due to our basic education being flawed.

Today we have come to such a state that people ask whether knowledge of religion is of help in their upkeep. This is a matter of shame. The *śāstras* admonish: "Do not ask whether Vedic education will provide you with food. We eat and live but to learn the Vedas." Your approach must be based on this principle. Today, a child born in a faith which has such high ideals is cut off from all opportunities of religious instruction at his very birth. Our concern is imparting worldly knowledge from the very start. Our children must be brought up properly and faith in God inculcated in them early in life.

Eternal

There are fixed periods for the four *yugas* or eons, *Krutha* (gold), *Tretā* (silver), *Dvāpara* (bronze), and *Kali* (iron). The four *yugas* together are called a *caturyuga*. A thousand *caturyugas* make one daytime of Brahmā and another equally long period is his night. According to this reckoning Brahmā is now more than fifty years old. Any religious ceremony is to be commenced with a resolve in which an account is given of the time and place of its performance in such and such a year of Brahmā, in such and such a month, in such and such a fortnight (waxing or waning moon), etc. From this account we know when the present Brahmā came into being. Even if we concede that he made his appearance millions and millions of years ago, he cannot be claimed to be *anādhi* (existing from eternity). How then can creation be said to have no beginning in time? When creation itself has an origin, how do we justify the claim that the Vedas are *anādhi*?

We learn from the *śastras* that the Vedas have existed even before creation. In fact, they say Brahmā performed his function of creation with the aid of Vedic *mantras*, which manifested as sound. To the modern mind this may not appear to make sense. But on careful reflection it will realized that the belief is based on a great scientific truth.

The *Paramātman*, being eternal, was present even before creation when there was no Brahmā. The Paramātman, or the Supreme Godhead, is eternal. The cosmos, all sentient beings and insentient objects, emerged from Him. The Paramātman did not create them Himself: He did so through the agency of Brahmā (the creative aspect of the Godhead). Through Vishnu (the sustaining aspect of the Godhead) He sustains them and through Śiva[1] (the destructive aspect of the Godhead) He destroys them. Later Brahmā, Vishnu, and Śiva are themselves destroyed by Him. The present Brahmā, when he becomes a hundred

Śiva, within a *linga* of flames, worshipped by Brahmā and Vishnu

years old, will unite with the Paramātman. Another Brahmā will appear and he will start the work of creation all over again.

Sound and Creation (Śruti)

The Vedas are called *Śruti* (Divinely revealed scripture). That which is heard is *Śruti*. The Vedas have been handed down orally from generation to generation and have not been taught or learned from any written text. That is how they got the name of *Śruti*. Why were these scriptures not permitted to be written down? Because the sound of the Vedas cannot be properly transcribed. There are sounds or phonemes that cannot be accurately represented in any script. Such sounds have to be learned by listening. In addition, there are *svaras* (tonal variations, proper accentuation) for Vedic *mantras*. Mistakes in enunciation are likely even if diacritical or some other marks are used in the printed text. Wrong chanting will not bring the desired results. There is much difference in the vibrations caused by pronouncing a syllable laying stress on it and pronouncing it without any stress. Correspondingly, there will be changes in our feelings and urges and the divine forces that rule nature. There is a story in the Vedas[2] which illustrates how wrong chanting can produce results contrary to what is intended. Tvastā, the divine carpenter, chanted a *mantra* with the object of begetting a son who would be the slayer of Indra. But he went wrong in the intonation of some syllables. So, unwittingly, he prayed for a son who would be slain by Indra instead of one who would slay that celestial. And his prayer (that had gone wrong in the intonation) was answered. When the wavelength shifts even minutely on our radio we receive the broadcast of a different transmitting station. Fine-tuning has to be done to get the required station. So is the case with the intonation of Vedic *mantras*. There should not be the slightest mistake in the *svaras*. Just as we receive a different station on our radio when the wavelength is changed, so the result is different when we make the wrong intonation.

This is the reason why it is of the utmost importance to learn the Vedas by listening—hence the name *Śruti*. Another explanation occurs to me for the name *Śruti*. The sages heard, did they not, the sound of the Divine vibrations that cannot be perceived by the common people? Did they read the Vedas in any book or did they compose them themselves? Neither. *Śruti* is an apt name for the Vedas since they were made known to the world after they had been first heard by the sages.

When the sages were meditating, the *mantras* of the Vedas appeared to them in a flash in their hearts. It may be that in this state of theirs they could neither see nor hear anything. The *mantras* must have appeared in a flash in the inner recesses of their minds.

It is further believed that the sages were able to hear the Vedas with their divine ears.

Arjuna wished to see the Lord's cosmic form. The Gītā has it that Krishna *Paramātman* said to him: "You will not be able to see my cosmic form with this eye of yours. I will give you a celestial eye...."

Standing Vishnu

Just as Arjuna was endowed by the Lord with a divine eye, the sages must have been invested with celestial ears to grasp the sound emanating from the *Paramātman* and pervading the vast space.

The vibrations of the Vedas serve the purpose not only of creation and the conduct of life. There are indeed Vedic *mantras* that help us to transcend this life and become one with the Ultimate Truth. When a man returns by the same way as he comes, does he not arrive at the starting point? In the same way when we go seeking how creation came about, we are led to the point where there are no vibrations, no movements, where there is utter stillness. Some *mantras* that create vibrations in our *nādis* (blood vessels and nerves) accomplish the same noble task of taking us to such a goal.

In sum, the Vedas are not anyone's compositions. The sages did not create them, nor were they inscribed by the *Paramātman* on palm-leaves.

Western Vedic Research

We may applaud European indologists for their research work, for making our *śāstras* known to a wider world and for the hard work they put in. But they were hardly in sympathy with our view of the Vedas. What is the purpose of these scriptures? By chanting them, by filling the world with their sound, and by the performance of rites like sacrifices, the good of mankind is ensured. This view the Western ideologists rejected. They tried to understand on a purely intellectual plane what is beyond the comprehension of the human mind. And with this limited understanding of theirs they printed big tomes on the Vedas to be preserved in the libraries. Our scriptures are meant to be a living reality of our speech and action. Instead of putting them to such noble use, to consign them to the libraries, in the form of books, is like keeping living animals in the museum instead of in the zoo.

Sound and Meaning

We may or may not know the meaning or significance of a religious rite, but we will be duly rewarded if we perform it in deference to the great men who have urged us to do it or because we follow the example of our forefathers who have done it. What matters is the faith inspiring our action. This applies particularly to worship through chanting *mantras* more than to anything else. The reason is that in such worship the proper voicing of the syllables of the *mantra* and the vibrations created

are what matter in bringing beneficial results. The meaning of the *mantras* comes later.

We must not refuse to perform a rite because we do not know its meaning, nor must we ask why we should perform what is prescribed in the *śāstras*. Conducting a ritual without knowing its significance, it occurs to me, is more important [than knowing the meaning of the words].

You may take it that this observation of mine has not been made in any seriousness. But, when I see that intellectual arrogance and deceit are on the increase and that the ignorant are being deprived of their one asset, humility, it seems to me that doing things in mere faith is to be lauded.

You must, in fact, be intellectually convinced about the need to perform a religious duty and, at the same time, you must be humble. The *mantras* are the laws of the *Dharmaśāstras*. If we knew their meaning we would be better able to live according to them.

The sound of the *mantras* does good to the man chanting them as well as to the listener by producing vibrations in the *nādis* (blood vessels and nerves) of both. As it fills the air it will be beneficent both in this world and in the next. This is the reason why the Vedas must be chanted with vigor, so that their sound reaches the utmost limits possible.

Yajna or Sacrifice

I spoke about the glory of the Vedas, about the features that contribute to their greatness as a scripture. One such feature yet to be dealt with is *yajna* or sacrifice.

Poornahuthi: concluding offering in a fire ritual

What is a *yajna*? It is the performance of a religious duty involving *Agni*, the sacrificial fire, with the chanting of *mantras*. The word itself is derived from the root *yaj* meaning "to worship", to evince devotion. The performance of a *yajna* is meant to please the *Paramātman* and various deities.

We have already seen the definition of the word *mantra*: that which protects us by being repeated and meditated upon. *Mananam* means repeating, turning over something in the mind. There is no need to vocalize the words of the *mantra*. Even if it is repeated mentally, healthy vibrations will be produced in the *nādis*. If the same—the Vedic *mantra*—is chanted loudly it will give divine joy to the listeners even if they do not understand its meaning. Such a sound has the power to make mankind happy.

Mind, speech, and body are dedicated to the Vedas when you repeat a Vedic *mantra* mentally and vocalize it outwardly during the performance of a rite involving the body. Of the Vedic rites of this kind *yajna* is the most important.

What is Advaita (Non-dualism)?

The Vedas proclaim that the one *Brahman*, call it the Truth or Reality, is manifested as so many different *devatās* or deities. Since each *devatā* is extolled as the *Paramātman* we know for certain that monotheism is a Vedic tenet. It is wrong to believe that the Vedas subscribe to polytheism merely because they speak of many deities. In doing so they mean that the one and only *Brahman* is revealed as many deities. It is for the conduct of the affairs of the cosmos that the *Paramātman* has created the various divine powers. These divinities are also in charge of the forces of nature, the feelings and urges of man. The Supreme Godhead has created them in the same way as He has created us. He fashioned us out of Himself—which means that He is also every human being.

This is the reason why non-dualism (*Advaita*) proclaims that the *Paramātman* and the *jīvātman* (the individual self) are one and the same. In the same way it is He who is manifested as the many deities. However, until we are mature enough to recognize the truth of non-dualism and realize it within, and until we reach the state in which we realize that we are not separate from the *Paramātman*, we have to perform rituals and help one another. In the same way the deities are also to be looked upon as separate entities and are to be worshipped through sacrifices. This is the law of the Vedas.

If we and all other creatures are to be happy in this world, we must have the blessings of the deities who govern the cosmic forces. It is for this purpose, to propitiate and please them for their grace, that the Vedas impose on us the duty of performing sacrifices.

If we attain *jnāna*, the wisdom to realize within ourselves the oneness of all, there will be no need for these deities. We may worship the *Paramātman* directly. However, so long as we make efforts to find release from this pluralistic cosmos, we have to worship the deities as separate entities.

The Threefold Purpose of Yajna (Sacrifice)

The Vedic sacrifices have a threefold purpose. The first is to earn the blessings of the deities so that we as well as all other creatures may be happy in this world. The second is to ensure that, after our death, we will live happily in the world of the celestials. But our stay in *devaloka*, the celestial world, is not for all time. It will last only until such time as we exhaust the merit earned by us in this world. The joy known in the celestial world is also not full or entire unlike the bliss experienced by great devotees and *jnānins*. It is nowhere equal to the bliss of

the *Ātmān* (the Self):[3] which is also described as "experiencing" *Īśvara* (the *Paramātman* with attributes).

Śankara has stated[4] that the joy that Indra knows is no more than a drop in the ocean of *Ātmānanda* or the bliss of Self-realization. However, life in the paradise of the celestials is a thousand times happier than life on earth with its unceasing sorrows. The second purpose of performing sacrifices is to earn residence in this paradise.

The third purpose is the most important and it is achieved by performing sacrifices, as taught by the Gītā, without any expectation of reward. Here we desire neither happiness in this world nor residence in paradise. We perform sacrifices only because it is our duty to invoke the blessings of the gods for the welfare of the world. In this way our consciousness will be cleansed, a pre-requisite for enlightenment and final liberation. In other words the selfless performance of sacrifices means that we will eventually be dissolved in the *Paramātman*.

Śankara, who has expounded the ideals of Self-realization and *jnāna*, says: "Chant the Vedas every day. Perform with care the sacrifices and other rites they enjoin upon you."[5] The *Ācārya* (the great teacher, in this case Śankara) wants us to conduct sacrifices not for happiness in this world, nor for the enjoyment of the pleasures of paradise. No, not for any petty rewards. Śankara exhorts us to carry out Vedic works without our hearts being vitiated by desire. This, according to his teaching, is the way to make our mind pure in order to realize the Self.

To Discover the One Truth

All Vedas have one common goal though there are differences among their adherents. What is this goal? It is the well-being of the entire world and all creatures living in it, and the uplift of the Self of each one of us and its everlasting union with the Ultimate Reality.

We may take pride in the Vedas for another reason also. They do not point to a single way and proclaim, "This alone is the path" nor do they affirm, "This is the only God" with reference to their own view of the Supreme Being. Instead, they declare that, if one adheres to any path with faith or worships any deity with devotion, one will be led towards the Truth. The scripture of no other religion speaks thus of the many paths to liberation. On the contrary, each of them insists that the way shown by it alone will lead to liberation. The Vedas alone give expression to the high-minded view that different people may take different paths to discover the one and only Truth.

A traditional portrait of Śankara

The Upanishads

In other countries philosophers try to apprehend the Truth on an intellectual plane. The Upanishadic inquiry is different, its purpose being to realize inwardly the Truth perceived by the mind or the intellect. Is it enough to know that halva is sweet? You must experience its sweetness by eating it. How are the Upanishads different from other philosophical systems? The Upanishads consist of *mantras*, sacred syllables, and their sound is instinct with power. This power transforms the truths propounded by them into an inward reality. The philosophical systems of other countries do not go beyond making an intellectual inquiry. Here, in the Vedas—in the *karmakānda* (the first part of the Vedas)—a way of life is prescribed for the seeker with actions and duties calculated to discipline and purify him. After leading such a life and eventually forsaking all action, all Vedic karma, he meditates on the truths of the Upanishads. Instead of being mere ideas of intellectual perception, these truths will then become a living reality. The highest of these truths is that there is no difference between the individual self and the *Brahman*.

It is to attain this highest of states in which the individual self dissolves inseparably in the *Brahman* that a man becomes a *sannyāsin* (ascetic who has renounced the world) after forsaking the very karma that gives him inward maturity. When he is initiated into *sannyāsa* he is taught four [principal] *mantras*, the four *mahāvākyas* (great *mantras*). The four proclaim the identity of the individual self with the *Brahman*. When these *mahāvākyas* are reflected upon, the seeker will arrive at the stage of realizing the oneness of the individual self and the *Brahman*. The four *mahāvākyas* occur in four different Upanishads. Many are the rites that you have to perform, many are the prayers you have to recite, and many are the ways of life you are enjoined to follow—all these according to the Vedas.[6] But, when it comes to achieving the highest ideal, the supreme goal of man, you have no alternative to the Upanishads and their *mahāvākyas*.

"The *Brahman* means realizing the *jnāna* that is the highest" (*Prajnānam Brahmā*): this is the first *mahāvākya*.[7] "I am the *Brahman*" (*Aham Brahmāsmi*) is the second *mahāvākya*.[8] "That thou art" or "the *Paramātman* and you are one and the same" (*Tat tvam asi*) is the third *mahāvākya*.[9] The fourth *mahāvākya* is "This Self is the *Brahman*" (*Ayam Ātma Brahmā*).[10]

In his most important text,[11] Śankara urges us to chant the chapters of the Vedas, perform the duties laid down in the Brāhmanas and, finally, to meditate on the *mahāvākyas* after receiving initiation into them, the purpose being our becoming one with the *Brahman*.

The Vedas find their final expression in the Upanishads. Indeed, the Upanishads are called "*Vedānta*". They form the final part of the Vedas in two ways. The Upanishads throw light on the meaning and purpose of the Vedas and represent the end of the scripture in more than one sense: while their text forms the concluding part of the Vedas, their meaning represents the Ultimate Truth of the same. The Upanishads are the summit of our philosophical [and metaphysical] system.

Upa-ni-shad means to "sit near by". The Upanishads are the teachings imparted by a guru to his student sitting by his side [sitting at his feet]. You could also take the term to mean "that which takes one to the *Brahman*".[12]

If a student sits close to the teacher when he is receiving instruction it means that a *rahasya* (a secret or a mystery) is being conveyed to him. Such teachings are not meant to be imparted to those who are not sufficiently mature and who are not capable of cherishing their value. What is held to be a secret in the Vedas is called a *rahasya*.

The Brahmasūtra (Basic Text for all Vedāntic Schools)

I said that every doctrine or system has a *sūtra* (text consisting of aphoristic statements), a commentary, and an elucidation of the commentary. The systems founded by Śankara and several other *ācāryas* belong to *Vedānta*[13] because they all cite the authority of the Vedas in support of their respective doctrines. Each of them has chosen the same ten Upanishads to comment upon according to their different philosophical perceptions.[14]

How is a *sūtra* to be understood? It must state truths in an extremely terse form. What is expressed in the least possible number of words to convey an idea or truth is a *sūtra*, an aphorism. According to this definition the Upanishads cannot be said to be *sūtras*. However, there does exist a basic text for all Vedāntic schools in the form of *sūtras*. This is the *Brahmasūtra*.

In the *Brahmasūtra*, on which there are commentaries according to the various philosophical schools, Vyāsa presents in an extremely terse form the substance of the ten (principal) Upanishads.[15] Who or what is man (the individual self)? What is the nature of the world (*jagat*) in which he lives? And what is the truth underlying all this? The *Brahmasūtra*, which is a basic text of all Vedāntic schools, seeks to answer these fundamental questions. Vyāsa does not project his personal views in his work. All he does is to make a penetrating study of the science of *Vedānta* that is already constituted by the Upanishads.[16]

All Hindu philosophical systems are based on the *Brahmasūtra*, but the *Brahmasūtra* itself is based on the Upanishads. That is why it has become customary to describe all Vedic schools of thought as "Upanishadic systems". When Westerners keep extolling our philosophy, chanting, "*Vedānta*! *Vedānta*!," they have in mind the Upanishads.

Veda and Vedānta: Are They Opposed to One Another?

The rituals mentioned in the first part of the Vedas (*karmakānda*) are sought to be negated in the second part (*jnānakānda*) of the same scripture. While the *karmakānda* enjoins upon you the worship of various deities and lays down rules for the same, the *jnānakānda* (path of knowledge) constituted by the Upanishads ridicules the worshipper of deities as a dim-witted person no better than a beast.

This seems strange, the latter part of the Vedas contradicting the former part. The first part deals throughout with karma, while the second or concluding part is all about *jnāna* (knowing or understanding). Owing to this difference, people have gone so far as to divide our scripture into two sections: the Vedas (that is the first part) to mean the *karmakānda* and the Upanishads (*Vedānta*) to mean the *jnānakānda*.

The Lord teaches us *Vedānta* in the Gītā and in it he lashes out against the *karmakānda*. It is generally believed that the Buddha and Mahāvīra (founder of the Jain religion) were the first to attack the Vedas. It is not so. Śri Krishna *Paramātman* (Krishna as the incarnation of the Transcendent Unity) himself spoke against them long before these two religious leaders. At one place in the Gītā he says to Arjuna: "The Vedas are associated with the three qualities of *sattva* (purity—the highest state), *rajas* (action, impurity), and *tamas* (darkness, inertia—the lowest state). You must transcend these qualities. Full of desire, they (the practitioners of Vedic rituals) long for paradise and keep thinking of pleasures and material prosperity. They are born again and again and their minds are never fixed in *samādhi* (absorption in the Infinite), these men clinging to Vedic rituals." In another passage Krishna declares: "Not by the Vedas am I to be realized, nor by sacrifices, nor by much study...."

Does not such talk contradict all that I have spoken so far about the Vedas, that they are the source of all our *dharma*?

With some thinking we will realize that there is in fact no contradiction. Would it be possible for us, in our present condition, to go beyond the three *gunas* (qualities of the phenomenal world) even to the slightest extent and realize the true state of the Self spoken of in the Upanishads? The purpose of the Vedic rituals is to take us, by degrees, to this state. So long as we believe that the world is real we worship the deities so as to be vouchsafed happiness. And this world, which we think is real, is also benefited by such worship. Thinking the deities to be real, we help them and in return we are helped by them. Living happily on this earth we long to go to the world of the celestials and enjoy the pleasures of paradise. So far so good. But if we stopped at this stage would it not mean losing sight of our supreme objective? Is not this objective, this goal, our becoming one with the *Paramātman*? Would it not be foolish to ignore this great ideal of ours and still cling to mundane happiness?

In our present state of immaturity it is not possible to think of the world being unreal. Recognizing this, the Vedas provide us the rituals to be performed for happiness in this world. Because of our inadequacies we are unable to devote ourselves to a formless *Paramātman* from whom we are not different. So the Vedas have devised a system in which a number of deities are worshipped. But, in course of time, as we perform the rituals and worship the deities, we must make efforts to advance to the state of wisdom and enlightenment in which the world will be seen to be unreal and the rites will become unnecessary. Instead of worshipping many deities, we must reach the state in which we will recognize that we have no existence other than that of our being dissolved in the *Paramātman*. We must perform Vedic sacraments with the knowledge

that they prepare us to go to this high state by making our mind pure and one-pointed.

If we perform rituals with the sole idea of worldly happiness and carry on trade with the celestials by conducting sacrifices (offering them oblations and receiving benefits from them in return), we will never come face to face with the Truth. Even if we go to the world of the celestials, we will not be blessed with Self-realization. Our residence in paradise is commensurate with the merit we earn here and is not permanent. Sooner or later we will have to return to this world and be in the womb of a mother. The ritual worship and other sacraments of the Vedas are to some extent the result of making an adjustment to our present immature state of mind. But their real purpose is to take us forward gradually from this very immature state and illumine us within. It would be wrong to refuse to go beyond the stage of ritual worship.

If, to begin with, it is not right to refuse all at once to perform Vedic rites, it would be equally not right, subsequently, to refuse to give them up. Nowadays, people are averse to ritual to start with itself. "What?" they exclaim. "Who wants to perform sacrifices? Why should we chant the Vedas? Let us go directly to the Upanishads." Some of them can speak eloquently about the Upanishads from a mere intellectual understanding of them. But none has the inward experience of the truths propounded in them and we do not see them emerging as men of detachment with a true awareness of the Self. The reason for this is that they have not prepared themselves for this higher state of perception through the performance of rituals. If this is wrong in one sense, refusal to take the path of *jnāna* from that of karma is equally not justifiable.

If one has to qualify for the B.A. degree one has to begin at the beginning—one has to progress from the first standard all the way to the degree course. One cannot naturally join the B.A. class without qualifying for it. At the same time, is it not absurd to remain all the time as a failure in the first standard itself?

In the old days there were many people belonging to the latter category (that is people who refused to take the path of knowledge and wished to remain wedded to the path of karma). Now people belonging to the former category predominate (that is those who want to take the path of *jnāna*, without being prepared for it through karma). During the time of Śrī Krishna also the majority clung to rituals. His criticism is directed against them, against those who perform Vedic sacraments without understanding their purpose and who fail to go beyond them. Unfortunately, this is mistaken for criticism of the Vedas themselves. The Lord could never have attacked the Vedas *per se*. After all, it was to save them that he descended to earth, again and again.

In keeping with his times, Krishna *Paramātman* spoke against people who confined themselves to the narrow path of karma. If he were to descend to earth again to teach us, he would turn against those who plunge into a study of the Upanishads, spurning Vedic rites. It seems to me that he would be more severe in his criticism of these people than he was against those who were obsessed with karma.

Graduating to the Upanishads without being prepared for them through the performance of Vedic rites is a greater offence than failure to go along the path of *jnāna* from that of karma. After all, one has to go through the primary and secondary stages of education before qualifying for admission to college.

The Vedas and *Vedānta* are not at variance with one another. The *karmakānda* prepares us for *Vedānta* or *jnanakānda*. The former has to do with this world and with many deities and its adherents are subject to the three *gunas*. But it is the first step to go beyond the three *gunas* and sever oneself from worldly existence. If we perform the rites laid down in the *karmakānda*, keeping in mind their true purpose, we shall naturally be qualifying for *jnanakānda*.

A question arises here. The sound of the Vedas and the sacrifices benefit not only the person who chants the Vedas and performs the rites but benefits all creatures. If such a person (the one who chants the Vedas and performs the rites) renounces the world and becomes a *jnānin*, what will happen to the world and its welfare?

The answer is: the *jnānin* (person following the path of knowledge) is in an exalted state of

Chandi homam: prayer to Goddess Devi offered through fire rituals

awareness and while being in it he does not have to perform any sacrifices or other rites to ensure the good of the world. His life itself is a sacrifice, a *yajna*, and through him the world will receive the Lord's blessings even if he looks upon it as unreal or as a "sport" of the Supreme Being. Why do people flock to a *jnānin*? Why do they fall at his feet even if he keeps himself aloof from them? It is because they receive his grace. Whether or not he wants to give any blessings, the Lord's grace flows into this world through him. In his very presence people feel tranquil and, sometimes, even their worldly desires are satisfied. A *jnānin*, who realizes within that there is no deity apart from himself, can give his blessings in greater measure than the deities themselves. So it is wrong to think that, since he does not perform sacrifices, he does not do anything for the good of the world.

To start with, we must perform the rites prescribed by the Vedas. But in this there must be the realization that they are but steps leading us to the higher state in which we will ultimately find bliss in our Self, a state in which there will be neither rites nor duties to per-

Homam formations

experience of the Reality in which there will be no need for these very Vedas. First, the flowers, and from them the fruit. Though the flower looks beautiful, the fruit emerges only when it wilts or falls to earth. A tree does not fruit before it flowers. In the same way, to plunge into *Vedānta* without first going through a life of Vedic discipline is neither wise nor in keeping with reality. It is equally wrong to remain confined to the *karmakānda* and refuse to make an effort to acquire Vedāntic knowledge: it is like wishing that we must have only flowers and no fruits. There must be a sense of balance, a sense of proportion, in everything we do.

When Vedic rites are performed in a spirit of dedication to *Iśvara* they will loosen your ties little by little, instead of keeping you bound to this world. If you perform rites to please the Lord, without expecting any reward, your mind will be cleansed and you will tran-

form. Similarly, to start with, the deities must be worshipped but again with the conviction that such worship serves the ultimate purpose of arriving at the point where we will recognize that the worshipper and the worshipped are one. Thus, to begin with, all differences in functions must be recognized and life lived according to them. Different divisions of people have different duties, and the customs and rites assigned to each are such as to help them in the proper discharge of those duties. But in the very process of maintaining such differences there must be the conviction within that ultimately there are no differences, that all are one.

If the Vedas are to be learned and chanted and if the Vedic rituals are to be practiced—and the Vedas must be learned and chanted even as the Vedic rituals must be practiced—it is because in this way we shall be led to that supreme

Pada pūjā: anointing the feet of the elders and revered people

scend the three *gunas*. This is the meaning and purpose of *yajna*. Is not the word understood in English as "sacrifice"? When an offering is placed in the fire we say "*na mama*" ("not mine"): it is this attitude of self-denial that is the life and soul of a sacrificial rite. Is it possible to retrieve what has been offered in the fire? Even if it were, it would soon disintegrate. In this way you must reduce your ego-sense to ashes, also your possessiveness (*ahamkāra-mamakāra*). One who performs a sacrifice without being conscious of such high ideals but with the purpose of petty gains like ascending to paradise—is he not a fool?

There is no contradiction between the *karmakānda* and the *jnānakānda*. In the *karmakānda* itself *jnāna* is given an elevated place and the limitations of karma are mentioned. The underlying idea is that we must graduate from the one to the other [from karma to *jnāna*].

Karma, however, is not the goal of the Vedas. You must go beyond the stage of performing Vedic rituals even if they be for such a noble purpose as that of creating welfare in the world, cleansing your consciousness, and propitiating the deities. You must rise higher to the plane where you will realize that nothing other than the *Paramātman* exists, that the phenomenal world is unreal, that there are no entities called deities (*devatās*) with an independent existence of their own, and that there is no "I". When you come to this state there will be no need for the Vedas too for you: this is stated in the Vedas themselves.

Upanishadic Commentary on the Nature of the Self

Śankara selected ten out of the numerous Upanishads to comment upon from the non-dualistic point of view. Rāmānuja, Madhva, and others who came after him wrote commentaries on the same ten Upanishads based on their own philosophical points of view.

The *Kena Upanishad*[17] contains a story about the *devas*. The celestials in their arrogance failed to recognize the Supreme Being whose crown and feet are unknown. Ambikā (a female incarnation of God) then appeared to give instruction in *jnāna* (knowledge) to

Indra, the king of the *devas* (celestial beings). She explained to him that all our power emanated from the one Great Power, from the one *Mahāśakti*.

What we see is the object and we who see it are the subject: the seen is the object, the seer is the subject. We can see our body as an object, we can know about it, know whether it is well or ill. It follows that there is an entity other than it that sees it, the subject called "we". That which sees is the *Ātman*. The subject called the *Ātman* cannot be known by anything else. If it can be known, it also becomes an object and it would further mean that there is another entity that sees: and that will be the true "we". The *Ātman* that is the true "we" can only be the subject and never the object. We may keep aside objects like the body and *experience* ourselves, the subject called "we", but we cannot *know* the "we". "To know" means that there is something other than ourselves to be known. It would be absurd to regard the

Ātman as something other than ourselves. The true "we" is the *Ātman*, the Self. "Knowing" it implies that that which knows it ("we") is different from that which is known (the Self). What can there be that is different in us from our true Self? What is it that is other than the Self that can know the Self? Nothing. We say "*Ātmajnāna*" which literally means "knowing the *Ātman*". But is the phrase, "knowing the *Ātman*", used in the sense of a subject knowing an object? No. "*Ātmajnāna*" means the Self experiencing itself, and that is how "*jnāna*" or "knowing" is to be understood. This is the reason why the *Kena Upanishad* says that "he who says that he knows the *Ātman* does not know it". It goes on: "He who says that he does not know knows. He who thinks that he knows does not know and he who thinks he does not know knows."

The *Katha Upanishad* comes next. This Upanishad contains the teachings imparted by Yama (god of death) to the *brahmacārin* Naciket. It begins as a story and leads up to the exposition of profound philosophical truths. The Gītā contains quotations from this Upanishad.

What I said just now about the subject-object relationship is explained in depth in the concluding part of the *Katha Upanishad.* How do we remove the ear of grain from the stalk? And how do we draw the pith from the reed? Similarly, we must draw the subject that is the Self from the object that is the body, says the *Katha Upanishad.* "Desire, anger, hatred, fear, all these appertain to the mind, not to the Self. Hunger, thirst, and so on appertain to the body—they are not 'mine'." By constant practice we must learn to reject all such things as do not belong to the Self by "objectifying them". If we do so with concentration, in due course we will be able to overcome the idea that has taken root in us that the body and the mind constitute the "we". We can then exist as the immaculate Self without the impurities tainting the body and the mind.

The *Katha Upanishad* compares the spiritual exercise of separating the Self from the body and the mind to that of drawing off the pith, bright, pure, and soft, from the reed. Before you is the spadix of a plantain. When it wilts do you also droop? Think of the body as a lump of flesh closer to you than this spadix of the plantain. This spadix is not the subject that is "we", but the object. On the same lines you must become accustomed to think of the body as an object in relation to the subject that is the Self. During our life in this world itself—during the time we seem to exist in our body—we must learn to treat the body as not "me", not "mine". *Moksha* or liberation does not necessarily mean ascending to another [heavenly] world. It can be attained here and now. What is *moksha*? It is everlasting bliss that comes of being freed from all burden. He who lives delighting in his Self in this world itself without any awareness of his body is called a *jīvanmukta*. The supreme goal of the Vedas and *Vedānta* is making a man a *jīvanmukta*.

Krishna *Paramātman* speaks of the same idea in the Gītā. He who, while yet in this world, controls his desire and anger before he is released from his body—he will remain integrated (in yoga) and achieve everlasting bliss. If you realize the Self, as an inner experience, while yet in this world, at the time of your death you will not be aware that your body is severed from you. The reason is that even before your death, when you are yet in this world, the body does not exist for you. So is there any need for what is called death to destroy it? There is no death for the man who has absolute realization of his body being not "he" (when you mention the body the mind is also included in it). Where is the question of his dying if he knows that the body is not "me" (that is "he")? The death is only for his body.

The man who has no death thus becomes *amruta* ("immortal"). Hymns of the Vedas also speak of such deathlessness. This idea recurs throughout the Upanishads.

The body, and the mind that functions through it, are the cause of sorrow. All religions are agreed that liberation is a state in which sorrow gives place to everlasting happiness. However, according to religious traditions other than *Advaita* (non-dualism), a man has to go to some other world for such bliss after his death. Śankara Bhagavatpāda establishes that true liberation can be won in this world itself if one ceases to identify oneself totally with the body and remains rooted in the Self.

We have two enemies who prevent us from reaching the state of *amruta* (deathlessness): according to the Gītā they are desire and anger.[18] The first is denoted by desire, or *kāma*, the second by anger (*krodha*). An Upanishad says that one who has no body (that is one who is not conscious of his body) is not affected either by desire or by anger. That is (it says): "If you wish to be free from the evils of desire and anger you ought to free yourself of your body right now when you are yet in this world."[19]

What do the Vedas Teach Us?

The Vedas speak of a variety of matters. What are the rites to be performed in a marriage? Or at a funeral? How best is a kingdom (or any country) to be governed? How must we conduct ourselves in an assembly? You will find answers to many such questions in the Vedas.

The Vedas tell you about the conduct of sacrifices, ways of worship, methods of meditation. How is the body inspired by the Self? What happens to it (the body) in the end? And how does the Self imbue the body again? We find answers to such questions in these sacred texts. Also we learn from methods to keep the body healthy, the rites to protect ourselves from enemy attacks. What then is the goal of the Vedas? After learning about, or knowing all other matters, by inquiring into them and by making an assessment of them, we are enabled to grasp that by knowing which we will know everything. That is the reason why the Vedas deal with so many branches of learning, so many types of worship, so many different works and so many arts and so many social duties. By applying the body in various rites we lose consciousness of that very body. By directing our thoughts to various branches of learning, by examining various philosophical systems, and by worshipping various deities the mind and the intellect will in due course be dissolved.

We are more conscious of our body when we are engaged in evil actions than otherwise. By thinking about evil matters the mind becomes coarser. Instead, if we perform Vedic sacraments and worship and chant Vedic *mantras* for the well-being of the world, the desires of the body and the mind will wilt. Eventually, we will develop the maturity and wisdom to gain inner vision. In this way we will obtain release itself. Release from what? From *samsāra*, from the cycle of birth and death. When we realize that the body and the mind are not "we" and when we become free from them—as mentioned in the Upanishads—we are liberated from worldly existence.

The purpose of the Vedas is achieving liberation in this world itself. And that is their glory. Other religions promise a man salvation after his departure for another world. But we cannot have any idea of that type of deliverance. Those who have attained it will not return to this world to tell us about it. So we may have doubts about it or may not believe in it at all. But the Vedas hold out the ideal of liberation here itself if we renounce all desire and keep meditating on the Self. *Moksha* then will be within our grasp at once. There is no room for doubt in this.

"You look for God thinking him to be far from you. So long as you are ignorant (that is without *jnāna*) he is indeed far from you. Even if you look for him all over the world you will not find him. He is in truth with you."[20]

When we look afar at the horizon it seems to us to be the meeting point of the earth and the sky. Suppose there is a palm-tree there. We imagine that if we go up to the tree we will arrive at the point where the earth and the sky meet. But when we actually arrive at the spot where the tree stands we see that the horizon has receded further. The further we keep going the further the horizon too will recede from us. "We are here under the palm-tree but the horizon is still far away. We must also go further to overtake it." Is it ever possible to overtake the horizon? When we were at a distance from the palm, the horizon seemed to be near it. But when we came to it the horizon seemed to have moved away further. So where is the horizon? Where you are there it is, the horizon. You and the horizon are on the very same spot. What we call "That"—the Lord, who we think is far away—is by your side. No, he is *in you*. "That thou art," declare the Vedas—He is you (or you are He).

Essence of Upanishadic Teaching

The essence of the Upanishadic message is the burning desire to be free from time and space. It would be in proportion to the extent to which we burn within in our endeavor to be free from the spatio-temporal factor that we will be rewarded with the grace of *Īśvara* and be led towards the fulfillment of the great ideal.

There is no need to go to the mountains or to the forest for instruction. Space and time teach us how to remain unaffected by events. All that we need do is to pray to the Lord and make an effort to develop the will and capacity to put happenings of the moment back in time and distant in space.

Nyāya (Science of Reasoning)

Rational Way to Know God

Nyāya (logic, the science of reasoning) gives rationalism its due place, but this does not lead to materialism or atheism.[1] Through intellectual inquiry, *nyāya* comes to the conclusion that, if the world is so orderly with so many creatures in it, all of them interlinked, there must be an *Īśvara* to have created it. *Nyāya* recognizes that there are areas that cannot be comprehended by human reason and that the truths that cannot be established rationally must be accepted according to how the Vedas see them. This means that *nyāya* takes every care to see that reasoning does not take a course that is captious and that it leads to the discovery of truth.

To examine something with the instrument of knowledge is to purify that very knowledge. It is also a means of obtaining intellectual clarity. When there is lucidity the truth that is beyond the reach of this very intellect will appear to us in a flash. In other words there will be an intuitive perception of the truth.

It is indeed commendable to have faith in the Lord and in the *śāstras* even without carrying out any intellectual inquiry. But are we able to have such complete faith that will take us across worldly existence? Instead of idling away one's time, without making any intellectual effort to discover the truth, would it not be better to keep thinking about things even if it be to arrive at the conclusion that there is no God? A person who does so is superior to the idler who has no intellectual concern whatsoever. Perhaps the atheist, were he to continue his inquiry, would develop sufficient intellectual clarity to give up his atheism. But the idler has no means of advancing inwardly.

We Need All Types of Knowledge

We must make good use of our brain and mind. Indeed, we must make them sharp as if by frequent honing so that they will help us in finding the truth. Why did Śankara master all the *śāstras*, all the arts, all the sciences, Śankara who thought the world was *Māyā*? Why did he ascend the *Sarvagnya pītha* (the seat of the all knowing)?

Advaita embraces even those *śāstras* that apparently do not speak about it. That is why I am speaking about all such *śāstras* even though I am called "Śankarācārya" (great teacher of the Śankara tradition). Non-dualism inheres in dualism, qualified non-dualism, Śaivism (worship of Śiva), Vaisnavism (worship of Vishnu) and so on. It enfolds even those systems that are critical of it. *Advaita* does not state that other systems are totally false. If it opposes them it is only to the extent needed to counter their argument against itself. It concedes them the place they deserve.

Purānās (Traditional Stories)

Magnifying Glass of the Vedas

The *Purānās* are the magnifying glass of the Vedas. The principles and rules of *dharma* that are briefly dealt with in the Vedas are enlarged or elaborated upon in them in the form of stories. A subject briefly touched upon may not make a deep impression on the mind. If the same were told as an absorbing story it would at once make an impact on the mind of the listener or reader.

The Vedas urge us to speak the truth.[1] "Follow *dharma*, live a life of *dharma*" is a Vedic injunction consisting of just two words.[2] The importance of the pursuit of *dharma* is explained through a long story in the *Mahābhārata*.[3] "Be one to whom the mother is a god"—"Be one to whom the father is a god":[4] these two admonishments are enlarged on, as it were, through the magnifying glass in the story of Śri Rāma. Such dharmic virtues as humility, patience, compassion, chastity, which are the subject of Vedic ordinances, are illustrated through the noble examples of men belonging to ancient times, women of hallowed reputation. By reading their stories or listening to them we form a deep attachment to the virtues and qualities exemplified by them.

All these men and women whose accounts are contained in the *Purānās* had to undergo trials and tribulations. We keep committing so many wrongs. But consider these Purānic characters who had to suffer more than we suffer. Indeed some of them had to go through terrible ordeals. However, by reading their stories we do not form the impression that adherence to *dharma* means suffering. On the contrary, etched in our minds is the example of men and women of great inner purity who in their practice of *dharma* stood like a rock against all difficulties and challenges. At the same time, we are moved by their tales of woe and thereby our own inner impurities are washed away. Finally, the glorious victory they achieve in the end and the fame they achieve help to create a sturdy bond in us with *dharma*.

Itihāsas (Two Great Epics) and Purānās (Traditional Stories)

For the learned and the unlettered alike in our country the *Rāmāyana* and the *Mahābhārata* have for centuries been like their two eyes, pointing to them the path of *dharma*. The two poetic works are not included among the *Purānās* and are accorded a special place as *itihāsas*.[5]

Purā means "in the past". That which gives an account of what happened in the past is a "Purānā", even though it may contain predictions about the future also. The term can also mean what was composed in the past.[6]

Illustration from the *Rāmāyana*

Vālmīki composed the *Rāmāyana* during the lifetime of Rāma. Vyāsa, author of the *Mahābhārata*, lived during the time of the five Pāndavas and was witness to the events narrated by him in his epic.

The Epics and their Greatness

The *itihāsas* (the epics) are so highly thought of as to be placed on an equal footing with the Vedas. The *Mahābhārata* is indeed called the fifth Veda.[7]

The stories of the *Rāmāyana* and the *Mahābhārata* are in the blood of our people, so to speak. Today not many read these epics, but forty or fifty years ago it was not so. If our people were then known in the rest of the world for their truthfulness and moral character, the most important reason for it was that they were steeped in the *Rāmāyana* and the *Mahābhārata*. In the old days Tamil *rājas* made gifts of land to learned men to give year-round discourses on the *Mahābhārata* in the temples. Until thirty or forty years ago people gathered in their hundreds to listen to the *pūśāri* (traditional story-tellers) tell stories from the *Mahābhārata* through song to the accompaniment of his drum. For common folks then the *pūśāri*'s performance was both "cinema" and "drama". Cinema and drama have their own ill effects but not the art of the *pūśāri*. By listening constantly to stories from the *Mahābhārata* people remained guileless, respecting such virtues as truthfulness and morality.

Illustration from the *Rāmāyana*

The bigger *Purānās* contain a number of independent stories, each highlighting a particular *dharma*. In the *itihāsa* or epic it is one story from beginning to end. In between there are episodes but these revolve round the main story or theme. In the *Purānās*, as mentioned above, each story speaks of a particular *dharma*, while in the *itihāsa* the main or central story seeks to illustrate all *dharmas*.

Why Differences among the Gods?

Each *Purānā* is in the main devoted to a particular *devatā* (celestial being). In the *Śiva Purānā* it is stated: "Śiva is the Supreme Being. He is the highest authority for creation, sustenance, and dissolution. It is at his behest, and under him, that Vishnu functions as protector. Vishnu is a mere *bhogin* (one who indulges in enjoyment and pleasure), trapped in *Māyā*. Śiva is a yogin and *jnāna* incarnate. Vishnu is subject to Śiva and worships him. Once when he opposed Śiva he suffered humiliation at his hands." Stories are told to illustrate such assertions.

In the *Vaishnava Purānās* you see the reverse. They contain stories to support the

Krishna in battle, illustration from the *Mahābhārata*

view that Vishnu is superior to Śiva. "Is Śiva a god, he who dwells in the burning grounds with spirits and goblins for company?" these *Purānās* ask.

In each *Purānā* thus a particular deity is exalted over others. It may be Subrahmānya (son of Śiva), Ganapati (Ganesh—the elephant-headed son of Śiva) or Sūrya (the sun god). Each such deity is declared to be the Supreme God and all others are said to worship him. When, out of pride, they refuse to worship him they are humbled.

Doubts arise in our minds about such contradictory accounts. "Which of these stories is true?" we are inclined to ask. "And which is false? They cannot all of them be true. If Śiva worships Vishnu, how does it stand to reason that Vishnu should adore Śiva? The *Purānās* cannot all of them be true. Or are they all lies?"

Logical thinking seems to point to the conclusion that all Purānic stories cannot be

Śiva and Pārvatī with their sons Ganesh and Kārttikeya

Deities from the temple in Halebid. *Top left*: Ganesh; *top right*: Śiva; *bottom left*: Hanuman; *bottom right*: Krishna true. But, as a matter of fact, they are. A deity that suffers defeat at one time at the hands of another emerges triumphant on another occasion. And a god who worships another deity is himself the object of worship at other times. How is this so and why?

The *Paramātman* is one and only one. He it is that creates, sustains, and destroys. And it is he who exfoliates as the many different deities. Why does he do so? He has not cast people in the same mold. He has created them all differently, with different attitudes, the purpose being to make the affairs of the world interesting by imparting variety to them. The *Paramātman* himself assumes different forms to suit the temperament of different people so that each may worship him in the form he likes and obtain happiness. This is the reason why the one and only *Paramātman* manifests himself as so many different deities.

Everybody must have firm faith in, and devotion for, his chosen deity. He must learn to believe that this deity of his is the *Paramātman*, that there is no power higher. That is the reason why each manifestation or form of the Supreme Godhead reveals itself to be higher than other forms or manifestations. It is thus that these other forms are shown to have worshipped it or suffered defeat at its hands. Altogether it means that each deity worships other deities and is in turn worshipped by these others. Also each god suffers defeat at the hands of other gods and, at the same time, inflicts defeat on them.

Those who are capable of looking upon all deities as the manifestations of the one and only *Paramātman* have no cause for exclusive devotion to any one of them. It is only when we think that one deity is separate from—or alien to— another that the question arises of giving up one for another. If we realize that all are the different disguises of the One Reality, the various gods and goddesses portrayed in the *Purānās*, with all the differences among them, will be understood to be nothing but the *līlā* or sport of the Supreme Being. It is the One alone that seems divided into manifold entities. This is to help men of various attitudes and temperaments. If this truth is recognized we shall be able to see the stories in the *Purānās*—stories that seem contradictory—in the true light.

Sūrya, from the temple at Konarak

DHARMAŚĀSTRA (SCRIPTURE ON CODE OF CONDUCT)

Realizing the Ideals of the Purānās

The noble characters who figure in the *Purānās* serve as an ideal for all of us to follow. When we read their stories we are inspired by their example and we ask ourselves why we cannot be like them ourselves, why we should not share their qualities. But, even if we wanted to emulate their lives, would we be able to live like them without deviating at any time from the high principles that they upheld?

Man by nature is always unstill: he cannot keep his mind quiescent even for a moment. Bhagavān Krishna says in the Gītā: "Not for a moment can a man remain still, without doing work". So one must know the right path for work. One must make one's mind pure, acquire the highest of qualities and, finally, transcending these very qualities, realize the *Brahman*.

How can we live according to the tenets of our religion? How can we wash away our sins and cleanse our Self? And what must we do to attain everlasting happiness? Is not our present birth a consequence of the sins we committed in our past lives? We have to free ourselves from them and be careful not to sin afresh. We must elevate ourselves, our mind and character, so that we are not embroiled in sin again. The purpose of religion is this, to ennoble us and turn us away from sin. But how?

Discussion among scholars

How do we live according to the teachings of our religion? We do not know how.

In our present condition, what do we claim to know? Perhaps a little bit of the *Rāmāyana*, the *Bhāgavata* and other *Purānās*. We learn about the religious life lived by the characters portrayed in these works. But neither the *Purānās* nor the epics deal with the rites in a codified form, nor do they contain directions for their proper performance.

The *Purānās* and the epics give a dominant place to devotion. Is it possible to be engaged in devotion all the time, or to keep singing the glory of the Lord day and night? Or, for that matter, to be similarly engaged in *pūjā* (ritual worship) and meditation throughout? No. We have a family to look after. We have to bathe and eat and we have so much other work to do—all this takes time. The remaining hours cannot be set apart for *pūjā*. It would all be tiresome and we have, besides, to do other good works. How do we get such information?

From the *Dharmaśāstra*.

The *Dharmaśāstra* contains practical instruction in our duties, in the rites to be performed by us. In the Vedas these duties are mentioned here and there. The *Dharmaśāstra* deals with them in detail and in a codified form.

There is an orderly way of doing things, a proper way, with regard to household and personal matters including even bathing and eating. The ordinances of the Vedas cover all aspects of life and to conduct ourselves according to them is to ennoble our Self. Whatever we do must be done in the right manner—how we lie down, how we dress, how we build our house. The idea is that all this helps our inner being. Life is not compartmentalized into the secular, worldly and the religious. The Vedic *dharma* is such that in it even mundane affairs are inspired by the religious spirit. Whatever work is done is done with the chanting of *mantras* and thus becomes a means of Ātmic progress. Just as worldly life and religious life are integrated, harmonized, so are the goals of individual liberation and common welfare kept together.

Freedom and Discipline

There are a hundred thousand aspects to be considered in a man's life. Rules cannot be laid down to determine each and every one of them. That would be tantamount to making a legal enactment. Laws are indeed necessary to keep a man bound to a system. Our *śāstras* do contain many dos and don'ts, many rules of conduct.

There is much talk today of freedom and democracy. In practice what do we see? Freedom has come to mean the license to do what one likes, to indulge one's every whim. The strong and the rough are free to harass the weak and the virtuous. Thus we recognize the need to keep people bound to certain laws and rules. However, the restrictions must not be too many. There must be a restriction on restrictions, a limit set on how far individuals and society can be kept under control. To choke a man with too many rules and regulations is to kill his spirit. He will break loose and run away from it all.

That is the reason why our *śāstras* have not committed everything to writing and enacted laws to embrace all activities. In many matters they let people follow in the footsteps of their elders or great men. Treating me as a great

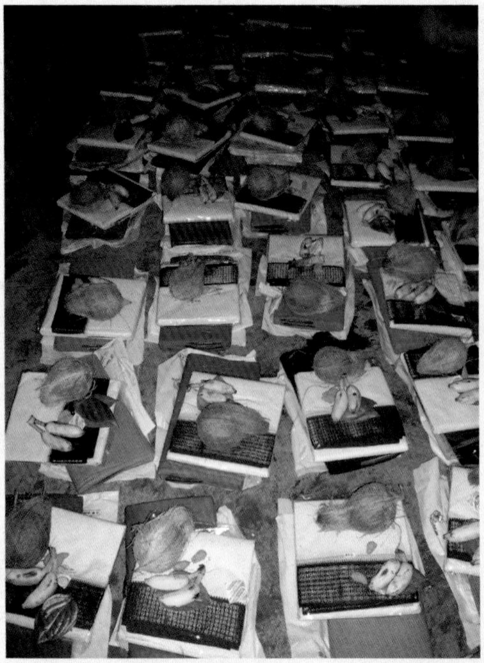

Gifts for *dampathi pūjā*

Dampathi pūjā: worshipping couples

His Holiness Śri Jayendra Saraswati performing Vyāsa *pūjā*

man and respecting me for that reason, don't you, on your own, do what I do—wear ashes, perform *pūjā*, and observe fasts? In some matters people are given the freedom to follow the tradition or go by the personal example of others or by local or family custom. Only thus will they have the faith and willingness to respect the rules prescribed with regard to other matters.

Setting an example through one's life is the best way of making others do their duty or practice their *dharma*. The next best is to make them do the same on their own by persuasion. The third course is compulsion in the form of written rules. Nowadays there are written laws for anything and everything. Anyone who has pen and paper writes whatever comes to his mind and has it printed.

Hindu *Dharmaśāstra* has come under attack for ordering a man's life with countless rules and regulations and not allowing him freedom to act on his own. But, actually, the *śāstras* respect his freedom and allow him to act on his own in many spheres. Were he given unbridled freedom he would ruin himself and bring ruin upon the world also. The purpose of the code of conduct formulated by our *śāstras* is to keep him within certain bounds. But this code does not cover all activities since the makers of our *śāstras* thought that people should not be too tightly shackled by the dharmic regulations.

The Forty Samskāras (Actions that Purify)

Samskāras (Actions that Purify)

The word *samskāra* means making something good, refining or purifying it. (*Sam*(*s*) = well; *kara* = making.)

The *Dharmaśāstras* (scriptures on *dharma*) deal with such *samskāras* as purify a man so as to make him fit to be united with the *Paramātman*. From the *Dharmaśāstras* we know in detail the forty *samskāras* that are to be performed by a man during his life's journey.[1]

Paradise or the Path of Ātmajnāna (Self-realization)

Our worldly existence is a mixture of joys and sorrows. Some experience more joy than sorrow and some more sorrow. Then there may be a rare individual here or there who can control his mind and keep smiling even in the midst of sorrow. On the other hand, we do see quite a number of people who have much to be happy about but who keep a long face. If a man lacks for something it means he is unhappy.

All creatures long for everlasting happiness. There are two abodes of eternal happiness. One is *devaloka*, the world of the celestials or paradise; the other is *Ātmajnāna*, the state of awareness of the Self (Self-realization). The *Ātman*, the Self, is bliss; it is the *Brahman*. To realize this truth is to attain everlasting blessedness. But this state, this joy supreme, is not experienced by the mind or the senses. It is the highest, the most exalted state and it transcends the senses and the mind; it is a state in which a man becomes aware that "the body is not I, the intelligence is not I, the consciousness is not I".

According to the Upanishads you will have eternal bliss if the senses and the mind are removed in the same way as you draw off the rib from a stalk of corn and remain just the *Ātman*. It needs great courage to pluck out the body and the senses realizing that "I am not the body. Its joys and sorrows are not mine". Such courage is not earned without inner purity. Conduct of religious rituals is meant for this, for purity of consciousness. There are forty *samskāras* to "refine" a man with Vedic *mantras* and to involve him in the rites associated with those *mantras*. These are the first steps towards the indissoluble union of the individual self with the Absolute—it is Advaitic *mukti*, non-dualistic release.

We must strive to become inwardly pure by the performance of daily rituals. Then, with the mind also cleansed, we must meditate on the Self and become one with It. This is the concept of Śankara. If a man has such a goal before him and keeps performing rituals throughout (that is even without becoming a *sannyāsin*) he goes to the *Brahmalōka* on death. During the great deluge when Brahmā is absorbed in the *Brahman* he too attains non-dualistic liberation, so says Śankara. But if a man performs rituals for the sake of rituals without keeping before him the goal of oneness with the *Brahman* he will be rewarded with paradise, but not the paradise that is eternal. Though the stay be brief he will enjoy greater happiness there than on earth. It is *samskāras* that earn a man heaven.

The Eight Qualities (Gunas)

The eight *gunas* or qualities are: *dhayā*, *kshānti*, *anasūyā*, *saucha*, *anāyāsa*, *mangala*, *akārpańya*, *aspruha*. *Dhayā* implies love for all creatures, such love being the very fulfillment of life. There is indeed no greater happiness than that derived by loving others. *Dhayā* is the backbone of all qualities.

Kshānti is patience. One kind of *kshānti* is patiently suffering disease, poverty, misfortune and so on. The second is forgiveness and it implies loving a person even if he causes us pain and trouble.

Anasūyā you know is the name of the sage Atri's wife. She was utterly free from jealousy: that is how she got the name which means non-jealousy. Heart-burning caused by another man's prosperity or status is jealousy. We ought to have love and compassion for all and ought to be patient and forgiving even towards those who do us wrong. We must not envy people their higher status even if they be less deserving of it than we are and, at the same time, must be mature enough to regard their better position as the reward they earned by doing good in their previous life.

Saucha is derived from *śuci*, meaning cleanliness. Purity is to be maintained in all matters such as bathing, dress, food. There is a saying often quoted even by the unlettered:

"Cleanliness makes you happy and it even appeases your hunger." To see a clean person is to feel ourselves clean.

In Manu's listing of *dharmas* that are applicable to all, *ahimsā* or non-violence comes first, followed by *satya* (truthfulness), *asteya* (non-covetousness; non-stealing is the direct meaning), *saucha* (cleanliness) and *indriya-nigraha* (subduing the senses or even obliterating them).

The fifth *Ātmaguna* (Divine quality) is *anāyāsa*. *Anāyāsa* means to have a feeling of lightness, to take things easy. One must not keep a long face, wear a scowl or keep lamenting one's hardships. If you lose your temper you will be a burden to yourself as well as to others. *Anāyāsa* is a great virtue. In many of our rituals there is much bodily exertion. When we perform [certain sacrificial rites] we have to remain without food until 2 or 3 in the afternoon. There is no end to the physical effort we have to put in to conduct a sacrifice. Here *anāyāsa* means not to feel any mental strain. Obstacles, inevitable to any work or enterprise, must not cause you any mental strain. You must not feel any duty to be a burden and must develop the attitude that everything happens according to the will of the Lord. We must learn to make light of all the hardships that we encounter in life.

What is *mangala*, the sixth *guna*? There is *mangala* or an auspicious air about happiness that is characterized by dignity and purity. One must be cheerful all the time and not keep growling at people on the slightest pretext. This itself is extremely helpful, to radiate happiness wherever we go and exude auspiciousness. It is better than making lavish gifts and throwing money about.

To do a job with a feeling of lightness is *anāyāsa*. To be light ourselves, creating joy wherever we go, is *mangala*. We must be like a lamp spreading light and should never give cause for people to say, "Oh! he has come to find fault with everything." Wherever we go

we must create a sense of happiness. We must live auspiciously and make sure that there is happiness brimming over everywhere.

Akārpañya is the next *guna*. Miserliness is the quality of a *krpana* or miser. *Akārpañya* is the opposite of miserliness. We must give generously and whole-heartedly. At Kuruksetra Arjuna felt dejected and refused to wage war with his own kin. In doing so, according to the Gītā, he was guilty of *kārpañya dosa*. It means, contextually, that he abased himself to a woeful state, he became "miserly" about himself. *Akārpañya* is the quality of a courageous and zestful person who can face problems determinedly.

Aspruha is the last of the eight qualities. *Spruha* means desire; a grasping nature. *Aspruha* is the opposite, being without desire. Desire is at the root of all trouble, all evil and, all through the ages, it has been the cause of misfortunes. But to eradicate it from the mind of men seems an almost impossible task. By performing rites again and again and by constantly endeavoring to acquire the Ātmic qualities one will eventually become desireless.

Tirumūlar goes a step further. "It is not enough," he says, "to be attached to *Iśvara* who is without attachment and be free from other attachments. You must be able to sever yourself from the attachment to *Iśvara* himself."

The Buddha calls desire "thirst". Intense desire for an object is *trishnā*.[2] His chief teaching is the conquest of desire.

Desirelessness is the last of the eight qualities. The first one, *dhayā*, is the life-breath of Christianity. Each religion lays emphasis on a particular quality, though all qualities are included in the teachings of the Buddha, Jesus Christ, the Prophet Mohammed, Guru Nanak, Zoroaster, Confucius and the founders of all other religions. Even if these qualities may not have been pointedly mentioned in their teachings, it is certain that none of them would regard people lacking them with approval.

Gunas in Practical Life

All religions teach people to be loving, to be truthful, and to be free from jealousy, desire, and greed. But our religion goes further by imposing on us the performance of various *samskāras* to acquire these qualities in practical life. There is no use in merely preaching, in asking people to be like this or that. A man must be kept bound to a system consisting of such works as would help him in practice to acquire the noble qualities expected of it. Our religion alone does this.

Other religions, it is claimed, teach love and desirelessness. But Hinduism, it is alleged, does not give any importance to such qualities and is, besides, ritual-ridden. This view is totally erroneous. In fact, our religion does more than others: while laying emphasis on the eight qualities, it imparts lessons to take people beyond them, to a state that transcends these very qualities. It also believes that merely talking about the qualities will serve no purpose. After all, we know, don't we, that we have to be virtuous, truthful, loving and so on? Still we find it difficult to live according to these ideals. What purpose is served if our canonical texts merely keep urging us again and again to acquire noble qualities? That is why, unlike other faiths which contain a great deal of ethical and moral instruction, our religion teaches ethics and morality only to the extent needed. But is that all? Without stopping with mere precept it tells us how we may—in actual practice—cultivate and acquire them. This it does first by telling us stories through the *Purānās* of virtuous people who obtained fame and of evil-doers who got ill fame. But it recognizes that such examples are not enough to provide the necessary inspiration, so it lays down a number of *samskāras* for the purpose of obtaining inner purity. Ours is the only religion that gives practical training in making people virtuous and in acquiring moral excellence. Instead of being proud of this fact is it right to feel that there is something lacking in our religion?

The first of the eight qualities is love which is the chief teaching of Jesus and the last of them is desirelessness which is the cardinal teaching of the Buddha.

Samskāras Performed by Parents

The *Samskaras* begin with *garbhadhana*, that is from the time of impregnation. *Samskaras* that follow, namely *pumsavana* and *simantha*, are for the life taking shape in the womb of the mother. On the birth of the child Jathakarma is performed and on the eleventh day *namakarana* (naming ceremony is performed). When the child is six months old it is time for *annaprasana*. The *samskaras* from *garbhana* to *namakarana* are performed by the parents. In *annaprasana* while the father chants the *mantras* it is the child who partakes the *anna* or food.

Any *samskāra* must be performed at the right time and by doing so we are absolved of our sins. To wash away the *pāpa* (sin) earned by us in the past we have to go through *samskāras* in which our body, mind. and speech are applied.

We think evil with our mind, tell lies with our mouth, and sin with our body also. Indeed we practice all kinds of deception. The wrongs committed by mind, speech, and body must be wiped away by applying mind, speech, and body to virtuous purposes. With the mind, *Parameśvara* (the Transcendent aspect of *Iśvara*) must be meditated upon; with the faculty of speech, *mantras* must be chanted; and with the body, noble deeds must be performed. It is from the time of the *upanayana* (first initiation into Vedic study) that one becomes mature enough to perform *samskāras* that bring together mind, speech, and body.

Our fathers did not perform any *samskāras*. So we may feel sorry that we have been deprived of the benefits that would otherwise have come to us. Let us not give room for our children to make the same complaint about us. Let us perform *samskāras* for our sake and theirs.

Why not All Samskāras for All?

Various rites are common to all *varnas* (castes). Only Brahmins (priestly caste), *Kshatriyas* (warrior caste), and *Vaiśyas* (merchant caste) have the *upanayana* ceremony. There is nothing discriminatory about this nor need there

be any quarrel over the same. People belonging to the fourth *varna* (*Sūdras*) do physical work to serve the world and in the process acquire inner purity. They will gain proficiency in their hereditary vocations only by learning them from their parents or grandparents. They do not require *gurukulavāsa* (study at the home of the guru) over some twelve years [as is the case with Brahmins] nor do they have to learn the Vedas. If they do so their work will suffer.

Upanayana is the first step taken towards *gurukulavāsa*. When a boy learns the Vedas he must have no ego-feeling. At home he has a lot of freedom. His father will not be able to discipline him because his affection will come in the way. That is why the child is to be brought under the care of a guru. Vocations that require physical effort are different from the pursuit of the Vedas. There is no room for intellectual arrogance in them or for the nursing of the ego. So such work may be taught at home by the father or some other elder in the family.

Ceremony of *upanayana*

Fire ritual during initiation of a youngster into Vedic instruction

Those who serve by doing manual work do not require to go through *upanayana* or *gurukulavāsa*. Certain special skills or the finer aspects of an art or craft that *cannot* be taught at home may be learned from a Brahmin teacher. The Brahmin is expected to be proficient in all arts, all subjects, but none of these is meant to be a source of his livelihood. His vocation is teaching and the chanting of the Vedas and the performance of Vedic rites.

There is a relationship between the *samskāras* prescribed for a man and his vocation and mental outlook. So it would be wrong to think poorly of certain *varnas* who do not have to perform certain *samskāras*. You may think it strange, but it is my view that it is those who have to undergo more *samskāras* than others that must have been thought of poorly. The idea is that these people need more rites to be rendered pure. Others are not in need of so many to be cleansed within. The larger the dose of medicine taken by a patient the greater must be his affliction.

None excels the sages in impartiality. They do not talk glibly like us of equality but they are truly egalitarian in outlook since they look upon all as one with *Īśvara*. The conduct of the world's affairs is such that it requires people following different vocations, doing different jobs, and with different mental qualities in keeping with them. It is in conformity with these differences and dissimilarities that the sages assigned the *samskāras* also differently to different people. There is no question of high or low among them.

(Student-Bachelorhood) Brahmacaryāśrama

Upanayana (Leading a Child to the Guru)

The *upanayana* of a boy is performed when he is old enough to understand things and to chant the *mantras*. During this ceremony he is asked to go begging for alms. "Bādham", he replies ("I will do so"). So, before his *upanayana*, the child must know enough Sanskrit to understand the meaning. When he starts learning at the age of five he will have a basic knowledge of Sanskrit by the time he is eight years old, the age fixed for the *upanayana samskāra*.

The world will stand to gain if eight-year-old children wear the sacred thread, have sufficient knowledge of Sanskrit, and chant the *Gāyatrī mantra* (a *mantra* regarded as the essence of the Vedas). Today things have so changed that godlessness is thrust into tender minds.

Upa = near; *nayana* = to take or lead (a child). Near whom or what is (the child) taken? Near the guru. That is what *upanayana* means. Who is a guru? One who has mastered the Vedas. There is one guru during the *brahmacaryāśrama* (student-bachelorhood) and another during the last *āśrama* of *sannyāsa*. The first guru is learned in the Vedas, while the second is one who has forsaken all including the Vedas. In the first *āśrama* you acquire *vidyā* (learning); in the last *āśrama* you realize *jnāna* (knowledge).

Upanayana is initiation into the *brahmacaryāśrama* while *samāvartana* is the completion of this stage of life. *Samāvartana* means "return". To repeat, from the *upanayana* to the *samāvartana* is student-bachelorhood or *brahmacaryāśrama*. *Samāvartana* thus denotes returning home on completing one's study of the Vedic discipline in the *gurukula*.

An entire *āśrama* or stage in life is set apart

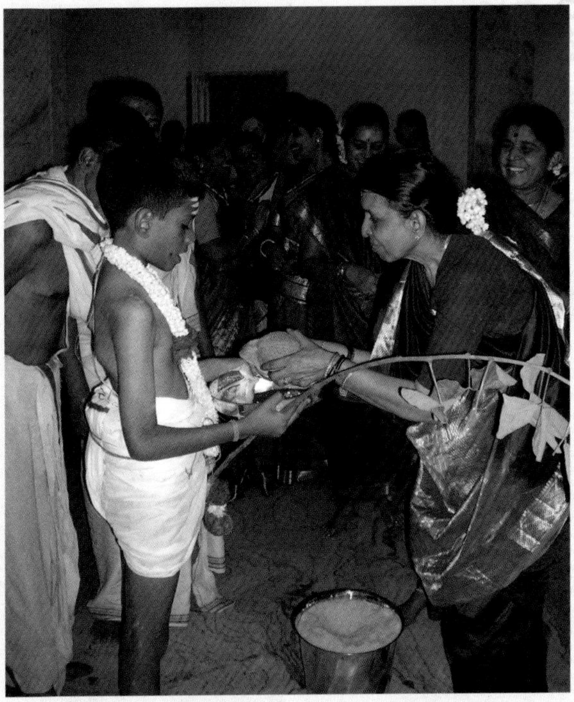

Brahmacārin seeks alms "Mother give me alms"

for the study of the Vedas: this is *brahmacarya*. The minimum period for student-bachelorhood is twelve years which is the time taken to master the Vedas.

Qualities of a Brahmacārin (Student-Bachelor)

Brahmacarya implies adherence to a number of rules with regard to food, the performance of rites, and the observance of religious acts of devotion. If a *brahmacārin* makes any mistake in chanting the Vedas, in the matter of tone or enunciation, he must do penance.

At mealtime the student can have his fill. The only restriction is that he must not give free rein to his appetite. He must beg for his food for such a practice makes him humble. The *śāstras* do not require him to fast. The student must be nourished properly during his growing years. But he must, at the same time, learn to develop pure and virtuous quali-

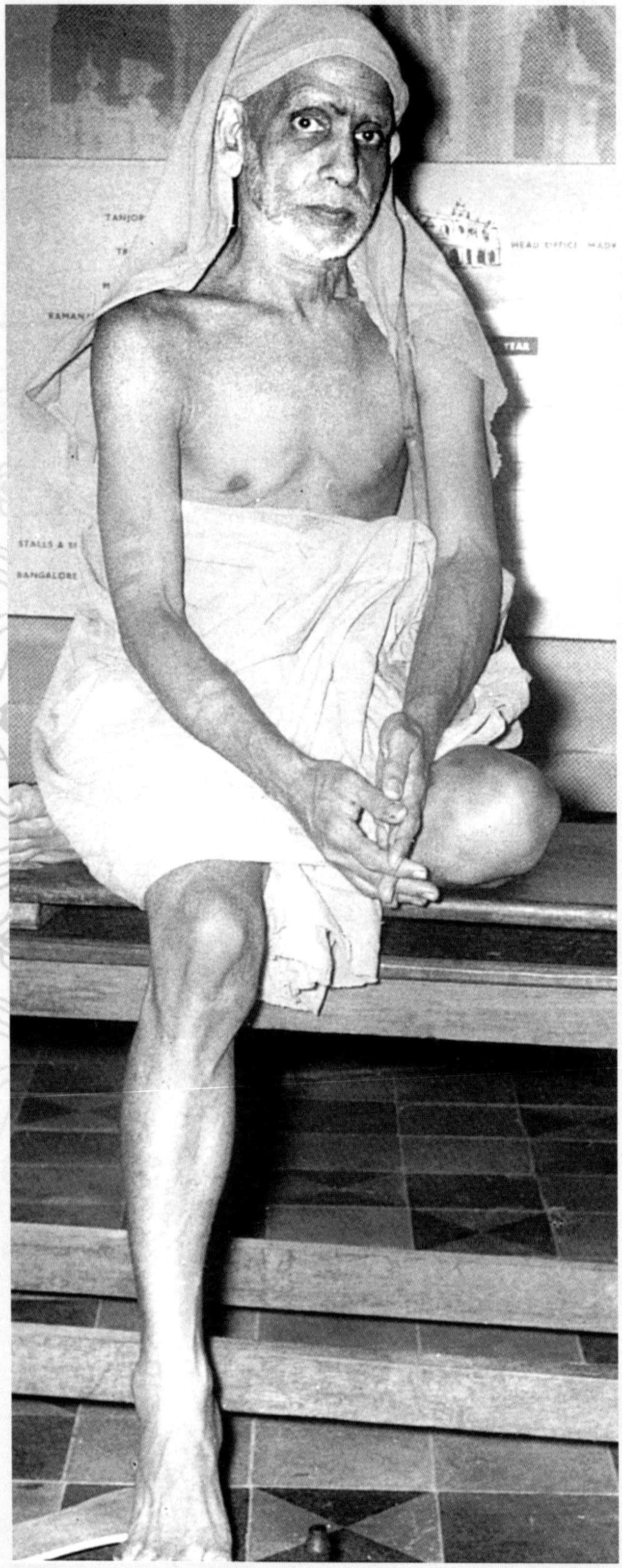

ties and there must be nothing rude or rough about him. It is by serving his guru that these qualities are inculcated in him.

During the twelve years in the *gurukula* the student must learn his recension of the Vedas. On completion of his stay in the *gurukula* he performs the *samāvartana*, returns home and marries.

Naishtika Brahmacārya (Lifelong Student-Bachelorhood) and Family Life

Our *dharma* takes into account the natural urges of man. The general rule is that, on his return home from the *gurukula*, the student must marry and settle down. It is difficult to go against the natural urges. But going along with nature does not mean being swept away in the flow of urges. After all, the goal of all our efforts is reaching the other shore—that is release from worldly existence. The householder must lead a life of *dharma* with his wife. But later he must become a forest recluse first and then, renouncing everything, a *sannyāsin*. This path to asceticism through stages is based on the fact that curbing the natural instincts forcibly is likely to be harmful. A person who decides in his youth to become a *naishtika brahmacārin* (lifelong student-bachelor) may later succumb to his natural passions. This would be an offence against the *āśrama* code of conduct and therefore sinful. As a householder he is not guilty of any offence if he goes by his natural urges within the constraints of *dharma*.

There are exceptions to any rule. Those who have firmness and maturity of mind and strength of character obtained from the *samskāras* performed in an earlier birth may become lifelong *brahmacārins*.

A person who has the light of knowledge in him and is free from passion must live in the forest giving up family responsibilities and performing only Vedic rites. He must leave his children and property behind and take only his wife with him to the forest. The wife, however, is not meant for carnal pleasure but is a partner in the conduct of rites involving the sacred fire—sacrifices, *aupāsana* (daily rites with the sacrificial fire), etc. This is the meaning of *vānaprastha* (forest dweller phase of life). A person qualifies for this stage of life when he is mature enough to leave home and hearth, children and relatives. Later he gives up the Vedic karma itself and turns his mind exclusively to the quest of the Self. This is the time when he enters the *sannyās-āśrama.*

The man who has thus separated himself from his wife and given up Vedic works is initiated into *sannyāsa* by his guru. He must constantly meditate on the *Paramātman* and experience the Truth as an inward reality. Also, he must have the realization that, "That Truth am I, all else is false play." Then he is by himself, beyond his body and mind, as the Ultimate Truth. This is *moksha*, liberation. Such a man will continue to dwell in his body until the fruits of his past karma are exhausted. But he will not be affected by such karma as a *sannyāsin* who has inward realization. From the point of view of the outside world he may still dwell in his body; but even in this state he is liberated. He is now a *jīvanmukta*. When the body perishes he becomes a *videhamukta* (liberated without the body). And he himself is now the unconditioned Ultimate Truth.

He who becomes a *sannyāsin* without having lived as a householder and he who becomes a *sannyāsin* after doing so, performing all the forty *samskāras* and acquiring all the eight Ātmic qualities, become alike the Ultimate Truth.

What is the fate of the man who does not become an ascetic but who keeps performing, until his death, all the *samskāras* and cultivates the eight Ātmic qualities? He is cremated on his death, is he not? After all, the majority of

people belong to his category. What happens to such people after their death?

Śankara does not state that they will dissolve in the Ultimate Reality. They do not have the intense urge, the burning desire, to grasp the *Brahman*, abandoning everything. If they have the all-consuming desire for the Truth, no force can hold them back from their quest. It is because they do not possess such a desire that they do not obtain non-dualistic release. However, they have faith in the *śāstras* and perform works according to them and contribute to the well-being of mankind and they are also thereby rendered pure inwardly. So, though they are not united with the *Paramātman*, they go to the presence of *Īśvara*, *Īśvara* who is the *Paramātman* with attributes (*Saguna Brahman*) and is behind the affairs of the world.

This is the same as the *Brahmāloka* (abode of Brahmā). In this there is no inseparable dissolution in the *Paramātman*, but the man who attains it remains in bliss "experiencing" *Īśvara*. Such a state is also to be described as *moksha*. There is nothing wanting, there is no sorrow, and there is the presence of the Lord. What more is wanted? This state is reached by those

who perform all the *samskāras* even though they do not become ascetics.

But one day *Īśvara* (the *Saguna Brahman*) will put a stop to the activities of all worlds and dissolve them in the great deluge (*mahāpralaya*). He will now become the *Nirguna Brahman*, the *Paramātman* without any attributes. At this time all those who reside by his side will unite with the *Paramātman* as the *Paramātman*, that is attain non-dualistic liberation.

In the great deluge all creatures—even those who have not performed any of the prescribed rituals, creatures like worms, reptiles, and so on also—will merge in the *Paramātman*. Then what is special about the one who unites with the Supreme Being after having performed all the *samskāras*? When the *Paramātman*, as the *Īśvara* with attributes, creates the worlds again those who do not perform the *samskāras* will be born again according to the karma of their past lives. Only those who have properly gone through the *samskāras* and been rendered pure will be inseparably united with the *Brahman*.

I have come far from the subject of *upanayana* (first ceremony to start Vedic study). I had sought an answer to the following questions: "Can a person remain a *brahmacārin* all his life? Can a *brahmacārin* become a *sannyāsin* without going through the stage of the householder?"

Domestic Life and Carnal Desire

Great men have spoken in the past about the evil done by carnal desire. Remarkably enough, our Vedic *dharma* has turned the same into an instrument for the purification of the Self by means of a *samskāra* and by imparting to it an element of propriety. It is not easy for an ordinary man to go to the forest and live as a recluse there or become a *sannyāsin*. To become mellow, he has to go through all the rough and tumble of life, experience all the joys and sorrows of his worldly existence. In the years of tenderness he must taste bitter, in boyhood or student-bachelorhood he must taste astringent, as an unripe fruit [in youth] he must taste sour, and as a mellow fruit [in old age] he must taste sweet. Ordinary people must go through all these stages so as to become mellow finally and to be filled with sweetness. What has not ripened naturally, or by itself, cannot be ripened forcibly. In this context one is reminded of the words of Rāmalinga Swamigal who speaks of a "prematurely ripe and withered fruit dropping". The sages knew that such would be the result if a man were forced into maturity by going against nature. The duties of marriage and the life of a householder are intended to make a person mellow naturally. Besides, are there not many beings that are to be born again as a consequence of their past karma? How can they be reborn in the absence of the *samskāra* called marriage?

The householder has to continue to chant the Vedas he was taught as a *brahmacārin*. He has also to teach these scriptures, perform a number of sacrifices and rites like *aupāsana* (daily rites with the sacrificial fire) and *sandhyāvandana* (morning and evening prayers).

The Brahmin must Keep his Body Pure

The temple called the body—it enshrines the power of the *mantras*—must not be defiled by any impurity. There is a difference between the home and the temple. In the home it is not necessary to observe such strict rules of cleanliness as in the temple. Some corner, some place, in the house is meant for the evacuation of bodily impurities, to wash the mouth, to segregate women during their periods. (In apartments it is not possible to live according

to the *śāstras*.) In the temple there is no such arrangement as in a house.

Wherever we live we require houses as well as temples. In the same way our body must serve as a house and as a temple for Ātmic work. The Brahmin's body is to be cared for like a temple since it is meant to preserve the Vedic *mantras* and no impure material is to be taken in. It is the duty of the Brahmin to protect the power of the *mantras*, the *mantras* that create universal well-being. That is why there are more restrictions in his life than in that of others. The Brahmin must refrain from all such acts and practices as make him unclean. Nor should he be tempted by the sort of pleasures that others enjoy with the body.

The Brahmin's body is not meant to experience sensual enjoyment but to preserve the Vedas for the good of mankind. It is for this purpose that he has to perform many rites. He has to care for his body only with the object of preserving the Vedic *mantras* and through them of protecting all creatures. Others may have comfortable occupations that bring in much money but that should be no cause for the Brahmin to feel tempted. He ought to think of his livelihood only after he has carried out his duties. In the past when he was loyal to his Brahminic *dharma* the ruler as well as society gave him land and money to sustain himself. Now conditions have changed and the Brahmin today has to make some effort to earn money. But he must on no account try to amass wealth nor must he adopt unśāstric means to earn money. Indeed he must live in poverty. It is only when he does not seek pleasure and practices self-denial that the light of Ātmic knowledge will shine in him. This light will make the world live. The Brahmin must not go abroad in search of a fortune, giving up the customs and practices he is heir to. His fundamental duty is to preserve the Vedic *mantras* and follow his own *dharma*. Earning money is secondary to him.

Gāyatrī (Invocatory Prayer) & Sandhyāvandana (Daily Prayer)

At least on Sundays, all those who wear the sacred thread must do *Gāyatrī-japa* (recitation of the *Gāyatrī māntra,* which is regarded as the essence of the Vedas) a thousand times. They must not eat unclean food, go to unclean places, and must atone for lapses in ritual observances and in maintaining ritual purity. Henceforth they must take every care to see that their body is kept chaste and fit for it to absorb māntric power.

Even in times of misfortune the *Gāyatrī* must be muttered at least ten times at dawn, midday, and dusk. These are hours of tranquility. At dawn all creatures including human beings rise and the mind is serene now. At dusk all must be restful after a day's hard work: that is also a time of calm. At noon the sun is at its height and people are at home and relaxed and their mind is calm. During these hours we must meditate on the *Gāyatrī*.[1]

Gāyatrī contains in itself the spirit and energy of all the Vedic *mantras*. Indeed it imparts power to other *mantras*. Without *Gāyatrī-japa*, the chanting of all other *mantras* would be futile. We find hypnotism useful in many ways and we talk of "hypnotic power". *Gāyatrī* is the hypnotic means of liberating ourselves from worldly existence as well as of controlling desire and realizing the goal of our birth. We must keep blowing on the spark that is the *Gāyatrī* and must take up *Gāyatrī-japa* as a religious act of devotion. The spark will not be extinguished if we do not take to unśāstric ways of life and if we do not make our body unchaste.

Gāyatrī-japa (invocatory prayer) and *arghya* (offering libation) are the most important rites of *sandhyāvandana* (daily prayers). The least a sick, weak person must do is to offer *arghya*, and mutter the *Gāyatrī* ten times. "Oh, only these two are important, aren't they? So that's all we will do, offer *arghya* and mutter the *Gāyatrī* ten times." If this be our attitude, in due course we are likely to give up even these that are vital to *sandhyāvandana*. A learned man remarked in jest about people who perform *arghya* and mutter the *Gāyatrī* only ten times, thus applying to themselves the rule meant for the weak and the unfortunate: "They will always remain weak and will be victims of some calamity or other." *Sandhyāvandana* must be performed properly during the right hours. During the *Mahābhārata* war, when water was not readily available, the warriors gave *arghya* at the right time with dust as a substitute.

Arghya must be offered before sunrise, at noon, and at sunset. These are the three times when you ought to offer *arghya*. By bathing in the Gangā your sins will be washed away.

Only by the intense repetition of *Gāyatrī* shall we be able to master the Vedic *mantras*. This *japa* of *Gāyatrī* and the *arghya* must be performed every day without fail. At least once in our lifetime we must bathe in the Gangā and go on pilgrimage to Setu.

If a man has a high fever, people looking

Pilgrims bathing in the Gangā (Ganges river) at Varanasi

Abhisekam: Sprinkling, anointing, bathing an image, king, or reverred person with water

after him must pour into his mouth the water with which *sandhyāvandana* has been performed. Today it seems all of us are suffering all the time from a high fever! When you run a high temperature you have to take medicine; similarly the *Gāyatrī* is essential to the Self and its *japa* must not be given up at any time. It is more essential to your inner being than medicine is to your body. *Sandhyāvandana* must be performed without fail every day. *Gāyatrī-japa* can be practiced by all of us without much effort and without spending any money. All that you require is water. *Sandhyāvandana* is indeed an easy means to ensure your well-being. So long as there is life in you, you must perform it.

Gāyatrī must be worshipped as a mother. The Lord appears in many forms to bestow his grace and compassion on his devotees. Mother loves us more than anybody else. We know no fear before her and talk to her freely. Of all the forms in which Bhagavān (incarnation of God) manifests Himself that form in which He is revealed as the mother is liked most by us. The Vedas proclaim *Gāyatrī* to be such a mother.

The *mantras* are numerous. Before we start chanting any of them, we say why we are doing so, mention the "fruit" that it will yield. The benefit we derive from the *Gāyatrī mantra* is the cleansing of the mind. Even other *mantras* have this ultimate purpose, but cleansing of the mind is the *direct* result of *Gāyatrī-japa* (recitation of the *Gāyatrī mantra*).

Even in these days it is not difficult to perform *sandhyāvandana* both at dawn and dusk. Office goers and other workers may not be at home during midday. [As a dispensation] they may perform the midday prayers 2 hours 24 minutes after sunrise.[2]

We must never miss the daily *sandhyāvandana* unless we find it absolutely impossible to perform. When we fall ill, in our helplessness, we ask others for water and food. In the same way, we must ask a relative or friend to perform *sandhyāvandana* on our behalf.

Let us all pray to the Lord that he will have mercy upon us so that the fire of the *mantras* is never extinguished in us and that it will keep burning brighter and brighter.

What About Women?

I said that the twice-born must perform *sandhyāvandana* with the well-being of women and other *jātis* in mind. I also explained why all *samskāras* are not prescribed for the fourth *varna* (*Sūdras*—manual laborers). Now we must consider the question of women, why they do not have such rituals and *samskāras*.

Even though we perform the certain ceremonies, including naming ceremonies, for new-born girls and celebrate their first birthday, we do not conduct their *upanayana* nor the other *samskāras* or vows laid down for *brahmacārins*. Of course, they have the marriage *samskāra*. But in other rites like sacrifices the main part is that of the husband, though she (the wife) has to be by his side. In *aupāsana* (daily rites with the sacrificial fire) alone does a woman have a part in making oblations in the sacred fire.

Why is it so?

What reason did I mention for the fourth *varna* not having to perform many of the *samskāras*? That these were not necessary considering their vocations and the fact that they can work for the welfare of the world without the physical and mental benefits to be derived from the *samskāras*. If they also spend their time in Vedic learning and in sacrifices, what will happen to their duties? So most of the *samskāras* are not necessary for them. They reach the desired goal without these rites by carrying out their duties.[3]

Just as society is divided according to occupations and the *samskāras* are correspondingly different, so too there are differences between men and women in domestic life. Running a household means different types of work, cooking, keeping the house clean, bringing up the children, etc. By nature women can do these chores better than men. If they also take an active part in rituals, what will happen to such work? Each, by serving her husband and by looking after her household, becomes inwardly pure.

In truth there is no disparity between men and women, nor are women discriminated against as present-day reformers allege. Work is divided for the proper maintenance not only of the home but the nation on the whole; and care has been taken not to have any duplication. There is no intention of lowering the status of any section in this division of labor.

The body, in the case of certain people, is meant to preserve the *mantras* and there are *samskāras* which have the purpose of making it worthy of the same. Why should the same rituals be prescribed for those who do not have such tasks to carry out? Glassware to be sent by railway parcel is specially taken care of since it is fragile. Even greater care is

Sumangali pūjā: married ladies worshipping

taken in dispatching kerosene or petrol. If the same precautions are not taken in transporting other goods, does it mean that they are poorly thought of? Astronauts are kept in isolation before being sent up in space and after their return. *Mantras* have their own radiation that is even more powerful than what is found in space. If you appreciate this fact, you will understand why Brahmins are separated from the rest and special *samskāras* prescribed for them.

The body of a Brahmin (male) is involved in the nurturing of *mantras*. So from the time of conception itself it is to be made pure through *samskāras*. There are *samskāras* with the same objective also after the boy child is born.

The vocations have to be properly divided for the welfare of mankind. If everybody paid attention to this fact, instead of talking of rights, it would be realized that the *śāstras* have not discriminated against women or any of the *jātis*.

The High Status of our Women

Those who complain that women have no right to perform sacrifices on their own must remember that men too have no right to the same without a wife. If they knew this truth they would not make the allegation that Hindu *śāstras* look down upon women. A man can perform sacrifices only with his wife. He does them for the well-being of all mankind and for his own inner purity. It is for this purpose that, after the *samāvartana* (return) following the completion of his student-bachelorhood, he goes through the *samskāra* called marriage.

Marriage is known as *saha-dharma-cārinī-samprayoga*. It means (roughly) union with a wife together with whom a man practices *dharma*. The clear implication is that carnal pleasure is not its chief purpose, but the pursuit of *dharma*. The *śāstras* do not ask a man to pursue *dharma* all by himself but require him to take a helpmate for it. The wife is called *dharma-patnī* (*dharma* partner), thus underlining her connection with *dharma*, and not with *kāma* or sensual pleasure. Here is proof of the high esteem in which the *śāstras* hold women.

An elderly Brahmin couple

The celibate-student and the ascetic alike follow the *dharma* of their respective *āśramas* (stages of life) not in association with anyone else. The householder has to conduct the karma as well as the *dharma* of domestic life with his wife as a companion, such being the rule laid down in the *śāstras*. The *dharma* of domestic life is their common property. Only a householder with a wife may perform sacrifices, not student-bachelors and ascetics. If the wife were meant only for sensual gratification, would the *Dharmaśāstras* have insisted that a man cannot perform sacrifices after her death? Women's libbers, who note that a woman cannot perform a sacrifice on her own, must also recognize the fact that the husband loses the right for the same without the wife and this is according to the Vedas themselves.[4] A great man lamented thus at the time of his wife's death: "You have taken away all my sacrifices as well as other rituals."

Our *śāstras* have thus given a high place to women in the matter of duties and works.

Marriage

For the Practice of Dharma

Dharma, *artha*, *kāma*, and *moksha* are the four aims of life. The first of them, *dharma* (proper code of conduct, set of duties), is a lifelong objective. The pursuit of *artha* (material welfare) and *kāma* (desire, love) must be given up at a certain stage in a man's life. But so long as such a pursuit lasts, it must be based on *dharma*. When a man renounces the world and becomes an ascetic, he transcends *dharma*, but he does not go contrary to it nor speak against it. Indeed, his life is governed by the *dharma* of *sannyāsa*.

All told, *dharma* is always a part of a man's life. When he reaches a high spiritual state, he may not be conscious of it, but *dharma* will abide in him and will keep shining as a light in all that he does.

The householder's stage of life commences with marriage. In it both material well-being and desire have their source in *dharma*. The student-bachelor and the ascetic are not concerned with the acquisition of wealth or carnal pleasure. The householder's stage of life, or *gruhasth-āśrama*, is a bridge between the two and in it both are permitted [within the bounds of *dharma*].

A man needs money and material goods to live in this world. As for *kāma* or carnal desire, it is needed so that children may be born according to their past karma. Until we have lived out our karma we too will have to be in this world. In this way if we want to give

A traditional wedding

The groom ties the sacred yellow thread on the bride

a "chance" to others, we have to earn money and experience *kāma* so that they [these others] may be born again. We need householders to feed *sannyāsins* who have given up karma. It would not be practical for all people in this world to become ascetics. The *śāstras* extol householders as the backbone of society since they live, or are expected to live, according to the dictates of *dharma* and fulfill the requirements of student-bachelors and ascetics.

After completing one's student-bachelorhood and acquiring learning and good qualities, one must marry so as to perform religious rites and live a life guided by *dharma*. Marriage is included among the forty *samskāras*, which fact shows that it is a sacred rite that sanctifies life. Just as *upanayana* is preliminary to the student-bachelor's stage of life, marriage is preliminary to that of the householder. Its purpose is disciplining the senses and the basis for the performance of various duties.

The householder's life is not to be taken to mean merely the enjoyment of sensual pleasure along with the carrying out of duties that mean good to the world. The fact is that the *śāstras* have formulated this stage of life in such a way as to make *kāma* itself instinct with *dharma*. *Dharma* means essentially bringing everything within certain limits, under a certain discipline and decorum. *Kāma* must be inspired by *dharma*, that is one must bridle one's passions in one's conjugal life, so that, step by step, the carnal urge will lose its keenness and eventually one will gain the mellowness to graduate to *sannyāsa*. That stage, though, comes later. But at first, even now, in the householder's stage of life, the passions have to be curbed, little by little, but not forcibly. In the *gurukula* (house of the guru) the celibate-student is brought under strict discipline. That saves him from being swept away by animal passion.

Make Marriages Simple

Girls today are sometimes married at the age of 25 or 30, far beyond the limit fixed by the traditional law. The inability to raise the money required for the wedding is one reason for this. All the ostentation at weddings, the dowry and other gifts given to the groom's people have no sanction in the *śāstras*. To demand a suit for the groom or a pair of boots, an expensive wrist watch or other luxury articles is nothing but extortion. It is as good as milking the bride's party dry. This kind of plunder is not approved by the *śāstras*.[1]

The words "the bride adorned with gold" occur in the *śāstras* relating to the marriage rites.[2] Gold symbolizes the grace of Laksmī (wife of Vishnu) but a *mangalasūtra* (auspicious string worn by the bride) with a grain of gold as part of it is enough. There is no need for other types of expensive jewelry, diamond studs, and so on. No silks are required. A cotton *sāri* will serve the purpose. Above all the custom of dowry must be scrapped.[3] There is also no justification in holding a lavish wedding dinner for the whole neighborhood. Nor is a music or dance recital needed.

Worshipping the father as guru

Gruhasth-Āśrama (Householder Stage of Life)

Gruhastha (Householder), Gruhinī (Wife of the Householder)

As I said before, after completing his student-bachelorhood a young man must take a wife for the pursuit of *dharma*. The latter should dedicate herself to him so as to become pure within. The purpose of marriage is a life of harmony and the procreation of virtuous children.

Gruha means a house. A young man who returns to his house from the guru's and practices *dharma* is a *gruhastha*. One who resides in a house, a *gruha*, is a *gruhastha*. The wife is called *gruhinī*, not *gruhastha*. The latter would mean no more than "one who resides in a house". But *gruhinī* means that the house belongs to her (the wife), that she manages the household.

Can a new Brahmin Caste be Created?

If I criticize Brahmins it is not because I feel that they cannot be corrected or that I have washed my hands of them. Nor do I think that Brahmins alone as a caste are responsible for all the ills of today. If I administer them a reproof now and then for their having given up their *dharma* during Islamic and British rule and for being lured today by the glitter of modern civilization, it does not mean that they are to be wholly blamed for everything. Placed as they are in today's circumstances any caste or class would have done the same. Those who find them guilty now think that they would acquit themselves better if they were in their place. But they too would have been compelled to make the same mistakes by the force of circumstances. If people hereditarily engaged in intellectual pursuits find themselves unable to apply their minds to Ātmic matters and instead become involved in mundane affairs, it means a topsy-turvy slide-down.

I do not justify such behavior nor the descent into worldly affairs from the heights of spirituality. Nowadays reformists try to justify even prostitution on psychological grounds. Similarly, I wish to point out that there is a psychological explanation for the degeneration of Brahmins also. If I criticize Brahmins, it does not mean that others should join in the attack, thinking that they (the Brahmins) alone are worthless people. It is the duty of these others to make Brahmins worthy of their caste. After all, during the past forty or fifty years, Brahmins have been an easy target of attack and ridicule. How silently they have suffered all this, also the humiliation at the hands of

Long unbroken stream of ghee offering accompanied by Vedic chants

their detractors. Until some four or five generations ago, Brahmins were the guardians of all our Ātmic wealth, all our arts. Considering this, is it not the duty of others to bring them back to the practice of their true *dharma*? They must be tactfully reminded of the high *dharma* they once pursued and the spirit of sacrifice for which they were known.

Unfortunately, what Brahmins did in the name of reforms resulted in the wrong kind of equality for, instead of raising people belonging to the lower strata to a higher level, it had the effect of bringing the upper classes downward. Equality can be of two types: in the first all occupy a high level in society; in the other all occupy a low level. To carry a load uphill is difficult but it is easy to push it down. Quality has suffered in the attempt to create equality. It is not desirable to have that kind of equality in which everybody does the same kind of work. Nor should it be thought that there is no equality in a system in which the various vocations, the various types of work, are divided among different groups of people. I have already spoken a great deal on the subject. Our endeavor must be to create unity in diversity, not uniformity.

It is important to remember that neither hatred of Brahmins nor dislike of Sanskrit has ever been a part of Tamil culture and civilization. Sanskrit is the repository of Ātmic and religious *śāstras*, a storehouse of poetry and works on arts. Everyone must learn to regard it as "our own language". The need for the existence of *Brāhmanya* (the ethos of the Brahmin way of life) as a separate entity must be recognized. This is essential to the preservation of the Vedas, the performance of sacrifices, etc, whose purpose is the good of mankind. Today the Vedas, the Upanishads and so on are available in print. Anybody can read them and try to understand them. But everybody need not learn to chant the Vedas; it takes many years to do so. Everybody need not also perform sacrifices.

There ought to be an element of humility on the part of those who wish to carry out reforms; there must also be sincerity of purpose. Then no need will arise to go contrary to the *śāstras*.

Aupāsana (Daily Rites with Sacrificial Fire) and Women

I said [in an earlier talk] that members of all castes must perform *aupāsana* (daily rites with sacrificial fire). The husband and wife must do it together. Even when the husband is away the wife must perform it by offering unbroken rice grains in the sacrificial fire. The Vedas themselves have given women such a right.

We hear people talk of "rights". It is my wish to create an awareness among women about their right, the right to *aupāsana*. I should like every home to become bright with the sacred *aupāsana* fire. Women should fight for this right of theirs and impress upon their husbands the importance of performing *aupāsana*. Women must make their husbands perform *aupāsana*. *Aupāsana* is indeed their one great Vedic "property".

Like *aupāsana, agnihotra* (fire sacrifice) must also be performed twice a day and must be performed with both husband and wife.

Sacrifices

Marriage is conducted with offerings made in the fire, is it not? *Aupāsana*, which must be performed every day, is commenced in this fire and it must be preserved throughout one's life. [Many rites] must be conducted in the *aupāsana* fire. The son lights his *aupāsana* fire during his marriage from his father's *aupāsana* fire. The son's *aupāsana* fire, like his father's, must be maintained throughout his life. Thus, without any break, the sacred fire is kept burning in the family generation after generation.

Varna (Caste) Dharma for Universal Well-Being

Jātis (Sub-divisions of Caste)—Why so many Differences?

There are four *varnas*—Brahmins (priests), *Kshatriyas* (warriors), *Vaiśyas* (merchants), and *Sūdras* (peasants, manual laborers). We identify *varnas* with *jātis*. In point of fact, *varna* and *jāti* are not the same. The *varnas* are only the four castes mentioned above. Within each caste there are many *jātis* (sub-divisions).

In common parlance *jāti* is used for *varna*. I am also using the two as interchangeable terms.

The *śāstras* lay down separate rites and practices for the four *varnas*. This means that within the fold of the same religion, Hinduism, there are numerous differences. Food cooked by one caste is not to be eaten by another. A young man belonging to one *varna* is not to marry a girl belonging to another. A vocation practiced by one *varna* is not to be practiced by another. The differences are indeed far too many.

Apart from the large number of divisions in each *varna* already existing, more and more divisions (or *jātis*) are coming into being. Thus Hinduism appears to be a strange religion.

Hindus today feel ashamed of the fact that a religion of which they have otherwise reason to be proud should have so many differences in it. Other religions too have their dos and don'ts. The Ten Commandments are meant for all Christians. So are the injunctions of the Koran for all Muslims. But in Hinduism the dos and don'ts are not the same for all. What one man does as part of his *dharma* becomes *adharma* (against the *dharma*) if done by another. For instance, it is *dharma* for one man to wear the sacred thread and chant the

Vedas, while the same is *adharma* for another. If the person who chants the Vedas does not bathe and keep his stomach empty he will be guilty of *adharma*. Another, however, need not necessarily bathe nor observe fasts.

Similarly, one must wonder at the fact that our religion is still alive in spite of all its differences and in spite of the fact that people are troubled by doubts about the same.

For some it is an offence to chant the Vedas, while for some others it is an offence not to chant the same. Why should there be so many differences in our religion and why should it seem to be discriminatory? Some feel that it is shameful even to speak about the differences and believe that they are a blot on our faith, which has otherwise many worthy features. While some Hindus try to satisfy themselves about these somehow, many find them to be a constant irritant. Then there are also people who feel angry about these differences and turn atheists as a reaction to the same.

Some are at heart proud of Hinduism but want the *varna* system to be scrapped and all Hindus to form a single class without any distinctions as is the case with the followers of other religions. "The Vedas must be thrown open to all and there must be one common form of worship for all", they declare. "We must do away with the system of separate religious rites and practices." Some go further and claim that such was the concept obtaining in our religion during the time of our forefathers. "The original thinkers of our religion who proclaimed the oneness of the individual self and the *Paramātman*," they argue, "would not have believed in such differences among the individual souls. Krishna *Paramātman* says in the Gītā that the vocations are assigned to people according to differences in their nature, not according to their birth." So they hold caste to be a blot on our religion and believe that the system of hereditary occupations did not originally obtain but was a later invention.

We must examine these views in some detail.

Innate Quality and Vocation by Birth

On the whole we see that the Lord functions on the basis that, whatever be the outward qualities of individuals, their inner quality is in keeping with their hereditary vocations.

How can birth be the basis of the quality on which one's occupation is based? Before a man's individual character develops, he grows in a certain environment, the environment evolved through the vocation practiced in his family from generation to generation. He adopts this vocation and receives training in it from his people. It is in this manner that his *guna* is formed, and it is in keeping with his work. Everybody must have the conviction that he is benefited by the occupation to which he is born. When people in the past had this attitude they were free from greed and feelings of rivalry. Besides, though they were divided on the basis of their vocations, there was harmony among them. Children born in such a set-up naturally develop a liking and aptitude for the family vocation. So what is practiced according to birth came to be the same as that practiced according to *guna*. Whatever the view of reformers today, in the old days an individual's ability to do a job was in accord with his *guna*; and in the *dharma* obtaining in the past a man practiced his calling according to his *guna*. Now it has become topsy-turvy.

What is the view of psychologists on this question? According to them, heredity and environment play a crucial part in determining a man's character, abilities, and attitudes. In the past all vocations were handed down from grandfather to father and from father to son. Besides, each group practicing a particular occupation or trade lived in a separate area in the village. The Brahmins, for instance, lived in their own quarter and, similarly, each of the other *jātis* its own quarter. So the environment also helped each section to develop its special skills and character. These two factors—hered-

ity and environment—are greatly instrumental in shaping a person's *guna* and vocation.

Vocations according to Guna (Character and Natural Inclination)—Not in Practice

What is the relationship between a man's vocation on the one hand and his *guna*—his character and natural inclination—on the other? If you pause to think about the question, you will realize that this relationship is highly exaggerated these days. Everybody suffers from a sense of self-importance and wants a great measure of freedom for himself in all things. That is the reason why people insist that their feelings and thoughts must be respected. They do not pause for a moment to consider whether such feelings are helpful to society, whether they are good or harmful for it. And, if they are harmful, should they not be checked for the sake of the community? Freedom is demanded for everything without such questions being taken into consideration.

A Wrong Notion about Brahmins

A wrong notion has gained currency that in the *varnaśrama* system the Brahmin enjoys more comforts than others, that he has more income, that he has to exert himself less than others.

In the order created by our *śāstras* the Brahmin has to make as much physical effort as the peasant. Since, at present, there is ignorance about the rites he has to perform, people erroneously believe that he makes others work hard and himself lazes about and enjoys himself. The Brahmin has to wake up at four in the morning and bathe in cold water, rain or shine, warm or cold. Then, without a break, he has to perform one rite after another and one of the twenty-one sacrifices. If you sit before the sacrificial fire for four days you will realize how difficult it is with all the heat and smoke. How many are the vows and fasts that the Brahmin has to keep and how many are the ritual baths.

Other castes do not have to go through such hardships. A Brahmin cannot eat "cold rice" in the morning like a peasant—he has no "right" to it. The *Dharmaśāstras* are not created for his convenience or benefit, nor to ensure that he has a comfortable life. He would not have otherwise imposed on himself the performance of so many rites and a life of such rigorous discipline. When he has his daytime meal it will be 1 or 2. (On the day of certain prescribed rites it will be 3 or 4.) This is the time the peasant will have his rest after his meal under a tree out in the field where he works. And the Brahmin's meal, mind you, is as simple as the peasant's. There is no difference between the humble dwelling of the peasant and that of the Brahmin. Both alike wear cotton. The peasant may save money for the future but not the Brahmin. He has no right either to borrow money or to live in style.

If daytime is divided into eight parts, the Brahmin may have his food only in the fifth or sixth part after performing all his rites. Before that he has neither any breakfast nor any snacks. And what does he eat? Not any rich food, no sweets like almonds crushed in sweetened milk. The Brahmin eats leafy vegetables growing on the banks of rivers, such areas being no one's property. Why is he asked to live by the riverside? It is for his frequent baths and for the leafy vegetables growing free there and for which he does not have to beg. He should not borrow money because if he developed the habit of borrowing he would be tempted to lead a life of luxury. Poverty and non-acquisitiveness (*aparigraha*) are his ideals. A Brahmin ought not to keep even a blade of grass in excess of his needs.

A Brahmin must not leave his birthplace and settle elsewhere. Honor or dishonor, profit or loss, he must live in his birthplace practicing his *dharma*. Nowadays, for the sake of money, people settle in England or America abandoning their motherland and their traditional way of life—and they are proud of it. Such a practice is condemned severely by the *śāstras*.

If all castes worked hard and lived a simple life there would be no ill-will among people and there would then be no cry that caste must be done away with. One reason for the "reformist view" is that today one caste is well-to-do and comfortable while another is poor and has to toil. Simplicity and hard work bring satisfaction and inward purity. Such a state of simple and happy life prevailed in our country for a thousand, ten thousand years.

I said that in these days vocations are not chosen on the basis of a man's qualities or natural inclinations. The only considerations are income and comforts. All people are on the lookout for all kinds of jobs and this has resulted in increasing rivalry and jealousy, not to speak of growing unemployment.

In the beginning, when vocations were determined on the basis of birth, everyone developed an aptitude for the work allotted to him as well as the capacity to learn it easily. This is no longer the case now. In the past a man's vocation was like a paternal legacy and he was naturally very proficient. Now there is universal inefficiency and incompetence.

The Eternal Religion

This religion has flourished for countless eons. What is the reason for its extraordinarily long history. If Hinduism has survived so long it must be due to some quality unique to it, something that gives it support and keeps it going. No other religion is known to have lasted so long. When I think of our religion I am reminded of our temples. They are not kept as clean as the churches or mosques. The latter are frequently whitewashed. There are so many plants sprouting from the *gopurams* (structures on top of the temples) and our temples support all of them. The places of worship of other religions have to be repaired every two or three years. Our sanctuaries are different because they are built of granite. Their foundations, laid thousands of years ago, still remain sturdy. That is why our temples have lasted so long without the need for frequent repair. We do so much to damage them and are even guilty of acts of sacrilege against them, but they withstand all the abuses. All are agreed that India has the most ancient temples. People come from abroad to take photographs of them. These temples still stand as great monuments to our civilization in spite of our neglect of them and our indifference. It is not easy to pull them down. Perhaps it is more difficult to demolish these edifices than it must have been to build them.

Our religion, to repeat, is like these temples. It is being supported by something that we do not seem to know, something that is not present in other faiths. It is because of this "something" that, in spite of all the differences, it is still alive.

The Fourth Varna (Śūdras) has its Own Advantages

The *dharma* of the fourth *varna* (*Śūdras*) involves much physical exertion and effort in its practice. Outwardly it may seem that its members do not enjoy the same status and comforts as others do. But we must note that they are comparatively free from the discipline and rituals to which the rest are tied down. In the past, they knew more contentment than the other castes, living as they did by the side of the Lord. Vyāsa himself says: "The age of *Kali* is in no way inferior to the other ages nor are *Śūdras* inferior to the other castes. *Kali* is in-

Śri Kamakshi Temple at Kanchipuram

deed elevated and *Śūdras* exalted."[1] In other *yugas* or ages Bhagavān is attained to (Self-realization) with difficulty by meditation, austerities, and *pūjā*, but in *Kali* He is reached by the mere singing of His names. The Brahmin, the *Kshatriya,* and the *Vaiśya* are likely to have self-pride, so they cannot earn Ātmic liberation easily. The Brahmin is likely to be vain about his intellectual superiority, the *Kshatriya* about his power as a ruler, and the *Vaiśya* about his wealth. So these three *varnas* will tend to stray from the path of *dharma*. A member of the fourth *varna*, on the contrary, is humble.

If a *Śūdra* does not have enough food to fill his belly, if he does not have enough clothing, and if he has no roof over his head to shelter him from rain and sun, the whole community

and the government must be held responsible—and both must be held guilty.

I repeat that the Brahmin's means of livelihood was in no way better than the *Śūdra's*, nor did he enjoy more comforts than members of the fourth *varna.*

Removal of the Ego

The *śāstras* are one with the socialists in proclaiming that all types of work are equally noble. If the socialists say so from the worldly or material point of view, the *śāstras* say the same from the spiritual point of view. To explain, since the well-being of mankind is dependent on the performance of a variety of jobs, there is no question of one job being inferior to another job or superior to it. If everybody does the work allotted to him thinking it to be an offering to *Īśvara*, all will be rewarded with inner purity, so say the *śāstras*. When work is accomplished in a spirit of dedication to God, the consciousness will be cleansed. And this, inner purity, is a means to becoming aware of the Self.

You may look at your work from two angles. One is from that of dignity of labor according to which principle no work is degrading. The second is from that of consecrating your work, whatever it be, to God. In either case "self-respect" has no place in it. If there is neither vanity nor ego-sense in doing one's duty or work, there will be no cause for anger, no reason to feel that one is assigned a particular set of religious practices that is humiliating. One should then be willing to accept the religious ordinances prescribed according to one's vocation. It must be noted that if a Brahmin enjoys bodily comforts in the same manner as a *Kshatriya* or a *Vaiśya*, his *mantras* will cease to be efficacious. If a laborer keeps fasts like a Brahmin he will not be able to do his duty, that is he will not be able to do physical work satisfactorily.

Today even intelligent people do not know the meaning behind different caste duties. "How can the work done by one man be according to *dharma* and meritorious while the same done by another is contrary to *dharma* and sinful?" they ask. In the old days, even unlettered people knew that it was a sin to adopt the vocation and duties of another *jāti* because it was injurious to society. They worked together during temple festivals and in carrying out public duties but in matters like food and so on they did not mix together since such mixing, they knew, was harmful to their traditional vocations. The mingling of castes, they realized, would damage the system of vocations, the system that was devised for the good of all society. For thousands of years all castes have lived according to this system, finding happiness and fulfillment in it. If they had not found such happiness and fulfillment, they would have surely rebelled against the system.

After the inception of British rule, Brahmins lost the royal grants of land but got jobs in the government. With the introduction of machines and increased urbanization, the handicrafts were destroyed and village life received a setback. While other communities found it difficult to get jobs, Brahmins were able to earn their upkeep without any physical exertion. This shook the very foundations of the system of four *varnas* and the British now used the opportunity to introduce the new principle of egalitarianism and the race theory. People lost their faith in the *śāstras* and with it there was a change of outlook. If, by the grace of *Īśvara*, the old system is restored, the work done by every individual—from the Brahmin to the *Pancama* (chief minister)—will bring inward purity to all. Besides, there will be the realization that each, according to his hereditary occupation, will contribute to the general welfare of mankind. If we pause to reflect on the subject, we will feel proud of *varna dharma* instead of being ashamed of it—and we will also develop a deep respect for those who created it.

A temple Gopuram

Cry "Grow"—Don't Cry "Perish"

It is important for all to become involved in a good cause, like the construction of a temple, or some public welfare scheme. Good feelings like love will surely spring in the hearts of people; at the same time much good will be done to society in general. Today, it is because people are not involved together in such [constructive] work that they turn their minds to destructive ideas, to argumentativeness, and to gossip and quarrels.

Unfortunately, some people think that if they inflame hatred between the communities or instigate quarrels or disputes, they will be able to gather a crowd of admirers round them. If we are all the time engaged in constructive work there will be fewer opportunities for trouble-making; indeed people will not find the time to do evil.

People go in procession until their legs ache, raising cries against this and that. Would there not be all-round growth and prosperity if all this manpower were employed to good work, if all the energies of people were turned to some constructive task? There is one type of "growth" that is higher than all others, it is the love that springs in the hearts of people. I think there must be a "tight" timetable for all: performing religious rites; worshipping at temples; listening to religious discourses; all castes working together for a divine cause or being engaged in social service. Adhering to such a timetable would mean universal happiness and prosperity. Besides, it would obviate the necessity of raising the cry of hatred against any caste.

We must regain the old sense of humility and modesty. If so, *jāti* will be confined to work, functions, and will not in the least be a cause of any feelings of differences. If all people adopt the same style of living that is simple and virtuous, there will be no cause for jealousy or heart-burning.

Whether or not we have the courage or the spirit of sacrifice to work towards this ideal, a way will open out for us if we at least recognize the ideal. May we have success in achieving this ideal with the blessings of *Ambā* (a female incarnation of God).

From Action to the Actionless State

Outward Karma—Inward Meditation

I have, in the course of my talks, dealt with a large number of religious rites. It may seem that the rituals and the service done to fellow men are meant for "others". But in truth they are meant for ourselves. By helping others, by serving them, by worshipping the Lord, we are rewarded with a sense of fullness. Others may really benefit from our help or may not. But when we serve them we experience inward peace and happiness—about this there is no doubt. What is called *paropakāra* (helping others) is indeed *upakāra* done to oneself (helping oneself).

In serving others we may have to undergo hardships, make sacrifices, and exert ourselves physically. But the happiness and sense of fullness we obtain is far greater compared to the trouble taken by us. The Lord does not have to gain anything from the *pūjā* we perform. In worshipping him, in reading the sacred texts, in going on pilgrimages, we find inward joy. Why do we perform *pūjā* and why do we help others? It is all for our own satisfaction.

Our affection for our wife, children, and others is in fact affection for ourselves. According to the Upanishadic teaching, it is for our own inner contentment that we love others. We perform *pūjā* to the Lord purportedly because of our devotion for him and we do social service presumably because of our love of mankind. But in truth the reason is we like ourselves and find happiness in such acts. For the sake of such happiness we do not mind encountering difficulties or making sacrifices.

To go in search of money, fame, and sensual pleasure, thinking them to be good, is to blacken our minds. What is it that is good for us? That which is good for the world—and it is but a form of the *Paramātman*. This truth is known to our inner being; we realize it deep in our mind. That is why we find greater fulfillment in doing good to others, unmindful of all the difficulties, than in finding comforts for ourselves.

The world is a manifestation of the *Paramātman* and so must we be too. We must remove the mirror called the mind and experience the truth within us that we are none other than the *Paramātman*. This is what is called meditation. All the work we do ought to lead finally to worklessness, to the meditation of the *Ātman*. The goal of all the sacraments I speak about is this.

Our actions make us happy in many ways. But in none of these actions do we find the peace that we enjoy during sleep. How we suffer if we lose even a single night's sleep? There is so much happiness in sleep. Do we not realize from this that the supreme "comfort" or happiness is worklessness. *Dhyāna* or meditation is the state of being absorbed in the *Paramātman*, a state of non-doing.

A Brahmin doing *japa*

Outward calm is the first step toward inward stillness—and this stillness is to be brought about in degrees and will not be gained all at once. That is why the wise tell us: "Reduce all your sensual activities. Do not join the crowd. Try to disengage yourself from all work including that of doing good to the world. Keep away from money and dwell in the forest." But do we listen to such advice? We shall do so only when our mind is cleansed.

That is why so many rituals are prescribed to purify the mind, the consciousness. It means that, instead of asking us *not to do* this and that, we are asked *to do* (perform) this and that rite. It is natural for us to be involved in some work or other. So, without any regard for our personal likes and dislikes, we perform the rites laid down in the *śāstras*. Even here our personal likes and dislikes will intrude but, unlike in the matter of meditation, we succeed to some extent at least in curbing them during the conduct of the rites. In due course, with the grace of the Lord, we will be able to perform good works without minding the discomfort and ignoring our personal likes and dislikes. Desire and hatred will be reduced and the mind will become pure. With the mind cleansed we will be able to perform one-pointed meditation. This is the time when we will be mature enough to forsake all works and become a forest recluse and practice meditation. If we are able to meditate with utter one-pointed meditation then everything will acquire the character of the *Paramātman*. There will be no need to leave everything and depart for the forest. Nor will it be necessary to speak of any religious discipline. The forest, the village, solitude and crowd—they are all the *Paramātman*. Both work and meditation are the *Paramātman*. Our inner peace will not be shaken by anything. We can remain still and tranquil and yet be all bustle outwardly.

In the beginning when it is not easy to control the mind and meditate on the *Ātman*, perform rituals. Then gaining mental purity through them, that is the rituals, forsake karma (work) and practice meditation, yoga, etc. Once perfection is attained in meditation and yoga, nothing will affect us. In this all is still inward, and yet outwardly there will be much activity.

Briefly put, this is the concept of *Bhagavatpāda* (Śankara): ultimately everything in the phenomenal world will be seen to be *Māyā* (cosmic illusion). The One Object, the One and Only Reality, is the *Brahman*. We must be one with It, non-dualistically, without our having to do anything in the same way as the *Brahman*. I, who bear the name of Śri Śankara, keep speaking about many rites, about *pūjā* (sacrificial offerings), *japa* (invocatory prayer), service to fellow men, etc. It is because in our present predicament we have to make a start with rites. In this way, step by step, we will proceed to the liberation that is non-dualistic. It is this method of final release that is taught us by Śri Krishna *Paramātman* and by our *Bhagavatpāda* (Śankara). At first karma, works, then *upāsana* or devotion and, finally, the enlightenment called *jnāna*.

If we advance in this way, by degrees, with faith and devotion, we will obtain the wisdom and mellowness for Ātmic meditation and inner control. Afterwards, we may keep doing any kind of work outwardly for the good of mankind.

What is the best means of practicing Ātmic meditation? We must be imbued with the tranquility that is from [one of the divinities] incarnate and remember every day [a manifestation of a divinity] in His quiescence. Let alone the idea of forsaking all works and becoming plunged in meditation. Let us also leave aside, for the time being, karma which itself is transformed into the high state of meditation. These are conditions to which we must rise at a later stage in our inward journey. But right now—at the beginning—let us train ourselves in the midst of our work to remain at peace and learn to meditate a little.

To start with, let karma, devotion, and meditation be practiced together. These are not opposed to one another but are complementary. In the end all will drop off one by one and the *samādhi* (absorption in the Infinite) of *dhyāna* (meditation) alone will remain. When we start our inward journey we must keep this goal of *samādhi* before us. So every day, leaving aside all other work, we must practice meditation for some time. But all the same we must not dismiss rituals as meaningless or as part of superstition. We must keep performing them. It is only when our impurities are washed away thus that we will realize the self-luminous Reality in us.

How to Cultivate Character and Good Conduct

How do we acquire character, how do we come to possess good qualities? By living according to the precepts of the Vedas and *śāstras* and by following the good customs practiced by our forefathers as well as by performing the rites that have been passed down to us. Good conduct springs from a good mind. So the mind must be free from evil.

Are we able to see ourselves in a soiled mirror? If we dust it and clean it well, we can see our reflection clearly. Even a clean mirror cannot produce a proper image if it keeps shaking. The mirror must be both clean and steady; only then will the reflection be true and clear. The mind, the consciousness, is like a mirror. The Supreme Being is the only Truth. When there are no evil thoughts in us, the mind-mirror will also be clean. If it is fixed on a single object it will remain steady—like a mirror that does not shake. Only then will the *Paramātman* be reflected in it.

Suppose a copper pot has remained immersed in a well for ten years or so. How much rubbing will it have to take before it becomes clean? The more we rub it the cleaner and brighter it will be. If our mind has been made impure with evil actions over many years it can be made chaste only by the performance of many a good deed, many a good work.

Is it enough to keep the copper vessel clean for today? What will happen to it tomorrow or the day after? It will become dirty again if it is not rubbed. Similarly, we must keep our mind ever pure by the daily performance of good works. In due course, a time will come when the consciousness will vanish and the Self alone will remain. Thereafter, there will be no need to cleanse the mind for the simple reason that there will be no mind to be cleansed. Until then we have to keep our mind pure through good actions and good conduct.

What is the Meaning of Worldly Existence?

"What is the purpose of my birth? Why was I born?" You must ask yourself this question again and again. You must also have some concern about whether you will reach the goal of your birth. "Why do we keep sinning?" is a problem that always worries us. "Why do we get angry? And why do we desire this and that? Can't we remain always happy without sinning, without anger and desire?" We do not seem to know the answers to these questions.

The fruit is formed from the flower, first in the tender unripe form and finally in the mellow form. The flower smells fragrant to the nose and the ripe fruit tastes sweet to the palate. The mellow or ripe fruit is full of sweetness. How did the fruit taste before it became ripe and sweet? The flower was bitter, the tender fruit was astringent, the unripe fruit was sour, and the fruit that is mellow now is sweet. Peace means sweetness. When there is peace all attachments sever themselves. When the heart is all sweetness all attachments disappear. There is attachment only so long as there is sourness. When you pluck an unripe fruit

from a tree there is sap in the stem as well as in the fruit. It means that the tree is not willing to part from the fruit and vice versa.

But when the sweetness is full, all the ties will be snapped and the fruit will drop to earth by itself. The tree releases the fruit or

Preparations for *pūjās*

the fruit frees itself from the tree. The separation is without any tears and happy [there is no sap]. Similarly, step by step, a man must become wholly sweet like a mellow fruit and free himself happily from the tree of *samsāra*, the cycle of births and deaths. Desire, anger, and so on, are necessary stages in our development like bitterness, astringency, sourness, and sweetness in the growth of a fruit.

When we are subject to urges like desire and anger we will not be able to free ourselves fully from them. But we must keep asking ourselves why we become subject to these urges and passions. We must constantly wonder whether they serve any purpose. If we do not remain vigilant about them we will become victims of their deception.

We should not, however, remain always in the same state as the one in which we find ourselves today, indifferent to everything. At the same time, when our bag of sins is still to be emptied, we cannot thirst for the supreme knowledge. Instead, let us keep doing our duty hoping that we will realize the supreme knowledge, if not now, after many a birth. Let us adhere to the *dharma* prescribed by the Vedas. If we do so, we will proceed gradually to the supreme *jnāna*. Now we are aware only of outward matters and outward disguises. So let us start with the outward rites of our religion and the outward symbols and signs. By degrees then let us go to the inner reality through the different stages—from that of the tender fruit to the fruit that is mellow and sweet.

Do We Need Rituals?

Some ask me whether religious functions, *pūjā*, etc, are not mere rituals. Ātmic awareness is an inward experience. As for rituals they are outward actions. The question is how rituals will help in experiencing the Self.

Rituals are indeed not necessary for one who has realized the Self. But we must put the question to ourselves whether we have truly realized It, whether we are mature enough for realization, whether we have become inwardly pure. Were we honest we would admit that we are far from having become mature for awareness of the Self. By taking many births, by performing many works, and by the habits of previous lives, we have concealed the bliss of knowing the Self. By conducting good rites, and by associating ourselves with noble objects, we have to banish the evil habits sticking to us from our past lives. Then there will be an end to karma itself and we will embark on Ātmic inquiry. Until then we have to perform what are called "mere" rituals.

The proper thing for ordinary people is to conduct all the rites mentioned in the *śāstras*. The benefits obtained from them may be seen in practice. When a person takes care to go through the rites strictly in the manner prescribed in the canonical texts, he will gain one-pointedness of mind. This should be of immense help to him in contemplating the Self later. And the desire to follow the *śāstras* in all aspects of life will mean that he will be brought under a certain discipline. When we conduct rites according to the *śāstras* our determination and will-power will be strengthened. Since we subordinate our views to the injunctions of the scriptures, we will cultivate the qualities of humility and simplicity.

So what do we gain by performing "mere" rituals? We will acquire one-pointedness of mind, discipline, non-attachment, will-power, humility. On the whole it will help us to live a moral life. Without moral conduct there can never be Ātmic inquiry and Ātmic experience.

The Starting Point of Yoga

People usually think that yoga means no more than controlling the breath and sitting stone-like. The literal meaning of the word is "joining", "uniting". All through our life's journey we have to join ourselves to various objects. But such joining is not permanent. That is why the mind remains unsteady. If we are joined to an object without the least possibility of being separated from it, it is yoga in the true sense. The root of the minds of all of us is the one *Paramātman*. Yogins control their breath to turn their mind to this prime root object. The root that gives rise to thoughts is the same as the root that gives rise to the breath. So if the breath is fixed on the root, the mind too will be absorbed in it.

Getting ready for the daily *pūjā*

Dharmas Common to All

How to Control the Mind

What is the obstacle to one-pointed meditation? The answer is the unstill mind. All problems are caused by the mind, by the desires arising in it. It is not easy to control the mind and keep it away effectively from desire. If we ask the mind to think of an object, it seems to obey us for a moment, but soon it takes its own course, wandering off. When I speak to you about meditation and tranquility, for a moment your mind will perhaps become still and you will be happy. But in a trice it will go astray and the calm you experienced for a few seconds will give place to unquietness.

If you bid your mouth to keep shut, it obeys you for a brief moment. Similarly, if you close your eyes asking them not to see anything, they shut themselves off from the outside world for some moments. But try as you might to tell your mind not to think of anything, it will not listen to you.

The mind must be kept under control. Thinking and non-thinking must be governed by your will. Only then can we claim that it is under our control, that we are masters of our consciousness.

There are two different ways of mastering the mind—the first is outward (*bahiranga*) and the second is inward (*antaranga*). We must have recourse to both.

The outward means consists, for example, of *sandhyāvandana*, sacrifices, charity, and so on. The best inward means is meditation. There are five inward (or *antaranga*) means to aid meditation. They are *ahimsā* (non-violence), *satya* (truthfulness), *asteyam* (non-stealing), *saucha* (cleanliness), and *indriya-nigraha* (subduing the senses, if not obliterating them). To practice *ahimsā* is to imbue the mind with love for all and not even think of harming others. *Asteyam* means not coveting other people's goods. For *satya*, or truthfulness, to be complete one's entire being, including body, mind, and speech, must be involved in its practice. *Saucha* is hygiene, observing cleanliness by bathing, maintaining ritual purity, etc. *Indriya-nigraha* implies limits placed on sensual enjoyment. "The eyes must not see certain things, the ears must not hear certain things, and the mouth must not eat certain things"—restrictions with regard to what you can see, listen to, eat, and do with your body. The body is meant for *sādhanā*, for Ātmic discipline. The senses must be "fed" only to the extent necessary to keep the body alive. These five *dharmas* are to be practiced by all Hindus without any distinction of caste or community.

Guru-Bhakti (Devotion to the Guru)

Who is God and what is His definition? In almost every religion, God is referred to as the Creator, the *Karta*, responsible for the creation and sustenance of the Universe. Since every effect must have a cause, it is inferred that there must be an ultimate cause, namely God, for the Universe. This is brought out in the *Brahmasūtra* by the expression *Karta śāstrā artha tvat* (*Īśvara* is the creator of the universe). Another definition of God is that He is the "dispenser of the fruits of our actions", be they good or evil—*Karmaphala-dāta*. The question may be asked why we should have *bhakti* (devotion) for a God who is the creator and dispenser. These are His self-chosen functions and He does them. Why should we have devotion to one who created, not at our request, and who dispenses, not according to our choice?

The *Yoga Sūtras* of Patanjali provide the answer. After defining Yoga as the control of mind's activity, the question of the way to control that activity comes up for consideration

and it is answered that this can be brought about by the worship of God, who is free from any imperfection or blemish, who remains unmoved and unmovable, who is the *stthānu* (Stable One), amidst the imperfect and the instable things of the world. Being the all-knowing Intelligence, God is not affected by anything which could distract the mind and prevent its control. It is such an ideal that we should have before us, to train ourselves in mind-control, so that the mind may be almost absolutely steady like a flame in a place where there is no breeze. Since concentrated meditation on a thing transforms one into the likeness of the thing meditated upon, meditating on God, who being omniscient is still unmoved and unaffected by want or desire, makes one like God Himself. As one holds fast to a steady pillar to prevent oneself from being tossed about, so too should one bind oneself through *bhakti* to God, to steady one's mind.

The purpose of prayer is not to petition for benefits. Such petitioning implies either that God does not know what we want, which will militate against His Omniscience, or that He waits to be asked and delights in praise, which will degrade Him to the level of ordinary man. Why then do we pray? Though Omniscient, God is immanent in every creature and knows what is in the heart of every person, yet, if what we wish to say in prayer remains unsaid, it afflicts our heart and so prayer heals that affliction. By prayer, we do not seek to change what God ordains; in fact, we cannot do so. We go to Him to remove our impurities. As Tiruvalluvar said, we attach ourselves to Him who has no attachments to rid ourselves of our attachments. A devout consciousness that God exists will itself do the miracle of alchemizing us into purity of nature. We obtain a spiritual charge into our frame by being in His presence.

Guru is *Iśvāra* in human form, but who is, however, free from the triple functions of creation, preservation and destruction, which pertain only to *Iśvāra*. If we have absolute faith in him, the guru will provide each of us an endowment for all of the devotion that we give to God. In fact, God is needed only when we cannot find a guru. *Guru-bhakti* is even higher and more efficacious than *Deva-bhakti* (devotion to any of thc manifcstations of God). Śri Vedānta Desika has declared that he does not consider God higher than the guru. According to a verse, when God is angry, the guru protects you; when the guru himself is angry, there is no protector in the world. If we surrender ourselves absolutely without any reservation to the guru, he will save us from all sorrows and show us the way to salvation. It is due to lack of *guru-bhakti* (devotion to the guru), that *Iśvāra-bhakti* (devotion to God) itself is waning in the hearts of men.

Ahimsā (Non-violence)

According to the *Manu-smriti, ahimsā* is the foremost among the *dharmas* that are common to all. It is included in the yoga of mind control. *Ahimsā* means much more than what is meant by non-injury; it implies not doing harm to others even by thought or word.

By nature none of us wants to cause any hurt to other people. But if others do us harm we want to retaliate in anger. Suppose one of our own children sets fire to our house in all innocence. We do not punish it but try to extinguish the fire and thereafter take care to see that the child is kept away from fire and other dangerous objects. We must learn to think that all those who cause us pain are like this child. If a person tries to hurt us, we must lovingly prevent him from doing so. We must not bear any ill-will against him nor think of retaliating. This is true *ahimsā*.

The practice of *ahimsā* contributes greatly to the yoga of mind control. The mind is like a demon. The mind will do us unlimited good if it is made subservient to us. Hanumān (the monkey god in the Rāmāyana) acquired his immense strength and was able to perform so many great and good deeds only because he had conquered his mind. The mind's power is immeasurable. All the cosmos is the work of the Supreme Goddess and in this creation of Hers even the mind of a tiny ant pervades the entire universe.

Many great men, many yogins, have stated that they were able to control their minds by adhering to true *ahimsā*. When we practice *ahimsā*, anger will naturally give way, the mind will become clear and will easily be controlled.

Thus if a man practices true non-violence (by body, mind, and speech), he will be rewarded with a benefit that he had not expected. In his presence all creatures will forget their ill-will and cease to cause hurt to any other creature.[1]

The minds of even cruel people will be transformed in the presence of men practicing utter *ahimsā*: in other words when a man is full of love he can make other people also loving.

"*Ahimsā paramo dharmaḥ*" (Non-violence is the supreme *dharma*). Buddhism and Jainism impose total non-violence on their followers. Not so our religion except in the case of ascetics. In Hinduism an exception to the general *dharma* of non-violence is made in the case of a righteous or just war and in a sacrifice in which sometimes animals are killed. It is to fetch the divine powers to earth and to appease them that animals are sacrificed in *yajnas*. It is our belief that the animals so sacrificed will attain to a high state that they cannot otherwise through their own efforts. Altogether it means the good of the animals and the welfare of the world.

In a war, heroes of the army sacrifice themselves in the cause of their nation. Is it not better to lay down one's life for the sake of others than fatten oneself doing nothing?

It is easy to claim oral allegiance to the principle of non-injury but difficult to practice the same. Quarrels and disputes are inevitable in the workaday world. In dealing with them action that is apparently violent may have to be taken. In reality such action is not to be regarded as violent. The intention or purpose is important here, not the action itself. Certain types of violence are justified according to the *śāstras* and not considered sinful, because such violence is committed not for our personal delight but in pursuance of our duty towards society: the offering of an animal in sacrifice, sentencing a murderer to death, killing an enemy in war.

If a religion makes the practice of non-violence universally applicable, there will be problems. Obviously, all cannot practice it at all times. So those who find it not practicable to follow the rule of *ahimsā* are made liable to sin. Our religion has taken a more realistic view on the question.

If a great *dharma* or principle is made common to all, in the end it is likely to lead to a situation in which no one will respect it in practice. In our religion—to repeat—the rule of absolute non-violence is meant only for *sannyāsins*. Without being bound by any śāstric injunction they have voluntarily adopted the principle and practiced it from generation to generation. Influenced by the example of the *sattva guna* (the mode of goodness, or a state of evenness, peace, and love) of ascetics these communities have become vegetarians on their own. And, following their example and without being compelled to do so, other castes too abstain from meat on days like the new moon, on the day of rites for our fathers, and days sacred to the various deities. When a principle is imposed only on a few, since it is difficult to make it universal, it becomes an ideal for others to whom it may not formally apply: they try to practice it as far as they can. Non-violence is a *sāmānya dharma* (a *dharma* common to all) in Hinduism. It is kept as an ideal though, on occasion, adherence to it is not practicable.

In the Vedic *dharma* the definition of *ahimsā* is the absence of ill-feeling in all action.

Truthfulness

Truthfulness means mind and speech being well integrated. The wise say that speech being at variance with the mind is untruthfulness.[2]

God has given man the gift of speech so that he may give expression to his thoughts and feelings. If what we speak is at variance with what we think (with our mind) God will take away the faculty of speech from us in our next birth—that is we will be born in the animal kingdom.

There are, as we have seen before, exceptions made in our *śāstras* to the rule of absolute non-violence: in waging a war to preserve *dharma*, in offering animals in sacrifice. Are there similar exceptions to the rule of truthfulness? You will perhaps say none. But, as a matter of fact, there are.

In any locality there must be a number of undesirable characters. Let us suppose that a certain citizen is annoyed with such characters and gives open expression to his anger. "He committed this outrage. That other man is guilty of such and such a crime", he keeps recounting the misdeeds of the bad elements. In doing so he is being truthful, that is his speech and mind are in accord. But by giving expression to his feelings no purpose is served, for neither he nor the community is benefited. It is a futile kind of accord—that of his speech and mind—and it cannot be called truthfulness.

Take the example of another person. He is full of evil thoughts and, if he gives expression to them, can he be called truthful? No.

So truthfulness, now we see, is not merely accord between mind and speech. It means voicing good thoughts, thoughts that are beneficial and are liked by people.[3]

Doing good through thought, word, and deed is truthfulness. All that does ill is untruthfulness. It is not enough that you speak to a man what is good for him. You must speak with affection and the one to whom your words are addressed must find them acceptable. If you speak harshly nobody will listen to you even if you mean well. Thus words that serve no purpose do not constitute a truth. Your speech must be beneficial and, at the same time, capable of bringing happiness to the man to whom it is addressed. This is truthfulness.

The wise say: "May he speak the truth. May his speech be pleasing. May he not speak the truth that is unpleasing. And may he not speak an untruth that is pleasing."

A mind that is subject to desire and anger will not give rise to words that bespeak affection and cause well-being. Truthful words that create good are the product of a mind free from desire and anger.

What is truth then? Thought and speech must be in accord; the mind must be serene; and the words spoken must be pleasing, that is, what is spoken must do good to the speaker as well as the listener.

To Serve Others is to Feel Blessed

A man can be fortunate in many ways. But there is nothing that makes him more fortunate than the opportunity he has of serving others.

When we serve our family we are not conscious of how we help it. We must learn to help people who are not our kin—other families, our village or home town, our nation, indeed all mankind. We have so many problems ourselves, we suffer so many hardships, and we have so many worries and cares. We must not, however, mind serving others in the midst of all our difficulties. We will forget our problems when we are immersed in the work of helping others. There is a saying: "Feed milk to your neighbor's child, your child will be nourished." The Lord will raise us up from our troubles as we do good to others. However, it is not with such considerations of profit that we must try to help people in difficulties. We must not worry about how others will benefit from our work, but consider how we will become naturally pure. Also, we must think of the happiness we will experience by serving our fellow men.

Service should not be confined to mankind but must be extended to the animal kingdom. In the old days ponds were dug exclusively for cattle and stone pillars were installed here and there for them to scratch themselves. Everyone must feed at least one cow every day with a handful of grass.[4]

There must be many others like us, many groups, who want to be engaged in social work. It should be ideal if the efforts of all were brought together under one body of like-minded members. Care must be taken that associations so formed do not break up; they must be managed honestly with a proper enforcement of discipline. Those who do philanthropic work must be men of courage and enthusiasm who take praise and blame equally.

We keep aloof from the outside world when we are ritually impure. We must regard any day on which we fail to do any service to others as a day of impurity. *Parameśvara* is the father of all creatures. By serving our fellow men we serve the Lord.

Towards Mental Purity

We can learn from the great men of our past who have left us lessons not only in Ātmic matters but in the conduct of family and social life. For instance, kinship and friendship in their time were based on high principles. When there was a marriage or obsequial ceremony all friends and relatives came forward to help. It was cultured behavior at its best and it was not based on any empty outward show. People then were truly and sincerely interested in helping the needy and the poor. At weddings they gave a little cash to the bride's parents, five or ten rupees, and the burden of those who conducted the marriage was lightened.

When everybody pays a little to the needy, the donor does not feel the pinch but the donee has a tidy sum with which to celebrate a marriage or perform an obsequial ceremony. Among relatives in the past there was not much gap between the rich and the poor. And the rich man helped his poor relatives. All this is part of *dharma*. The man who helps purifies himself more than the man who is helped.

Now things have changed. The well-to-do do not help their poor relatives. *Annadāna* (gift of food) was part of the noble tradition of the past. How is it today? At present too the well-to-do feed people, but with this difference that those fed are also well-to-do like them. When they give parties, banquets, etc., a great deal of money and material is spent in this manner. Where is the room for *dharma* or mental purity in all this? A party is given not with any noble intention but to promote one's selfish interests. The man who gives it thinks that he is practicing deception on the invitees. But the invitees, however, know that the host has no true feelings of affection for them. The host and the guest thus deceive one another. Altogether parties and toasts are nothing but a part of the modern art of deception and have nothing to do with the cleansing of the mind.

If you help a poor man with food or material, you and he are equally happy: there is affection on both sides. In parties, on the contrary, there is even ill-will. Hatred and resentment are caused in the hearts of have-nots by the parties given by the haves [for the haves]. Among relatives there should be no distinction between rich and poor.

You must not think that only the affluent can help the poor and earn merit. If you are not well off you may serve others by helping them physically. All of you in a locality may join together to dig a pond. All this contributes to inner purity. How do you deserve the grace of *Īśvara*? By constantly serving others, by being compassionate to all creatures. Your mind, your consciousness, will also become clear. In this pure consciousness of yours you will see the image of the Lord. Do you see any image in turbid water? We have made our minds muddy with impurities. We must make them limpid by being devoted to the Lord and by serving mankind. Then *Īśvara* will be within our grasp.

Fault-finding

"Do not magnify the faults of others", say the wise. "But if there is something good about a man speak appreciatively about it." I myself, however, am bringing your faults into the open. But, to repeat, you must not bring to light the drawbacks of others but only their good qualities.

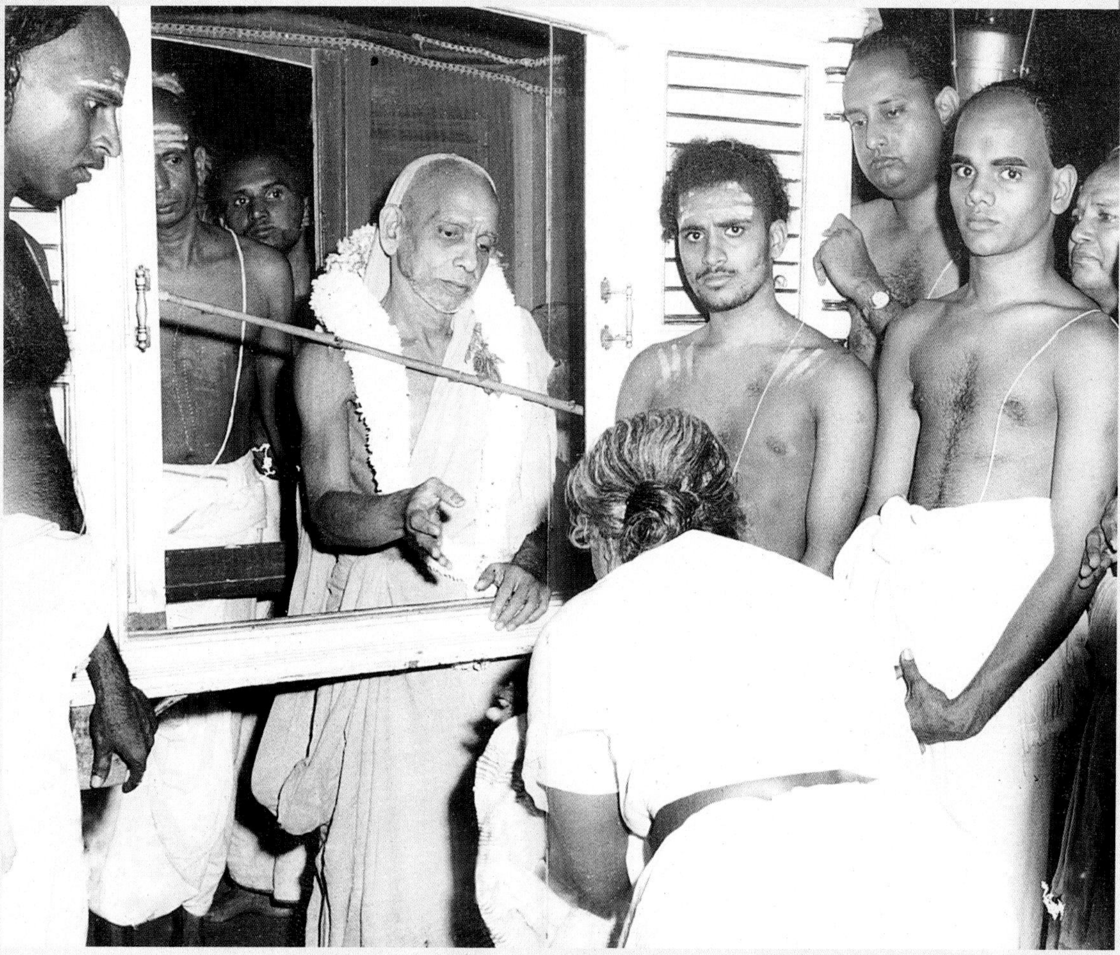

Pointing a finger at the faults of others or exaggerating them in speech and writing has become the practice today. The more learned a man is, the more eager he is to find fault with others. "Finding fault is indeed the work of a *doshajna*", it is said. But a *doshajna* is one who knows the faults of something or somebody, not one who reveals them to the world or exaggerates them. If you think a person has any drawbacks you must speak to him about them in a friendly manner [so that he may correct himself] but not constantly harp on them and expose them to the outside world.

We must be worthy enough to speak about the faults of others and we cannot take upon ourselves the role of an adviser when we need to correct ourselves. Advice given by us then would be counterproductive. If we tell a man what is wrong about him he might even feel boastful about it. When are we fit to advise others? When we are worthy enough and when we know that our word will have the desired effect.

Anger

It is customary to speak of *kāma* (desire) and *krodha* (anger) together. Krishna *Paramātman* says in the Gītā that desire and anger goad a man into sinful action.

When we intensely desire an object we try to get it by fair means or foul. It is a deadly enemy, desire: it eggs us on to commit sin. Equally deadly is anger. When we fail to get the object of our desire we turn our anger

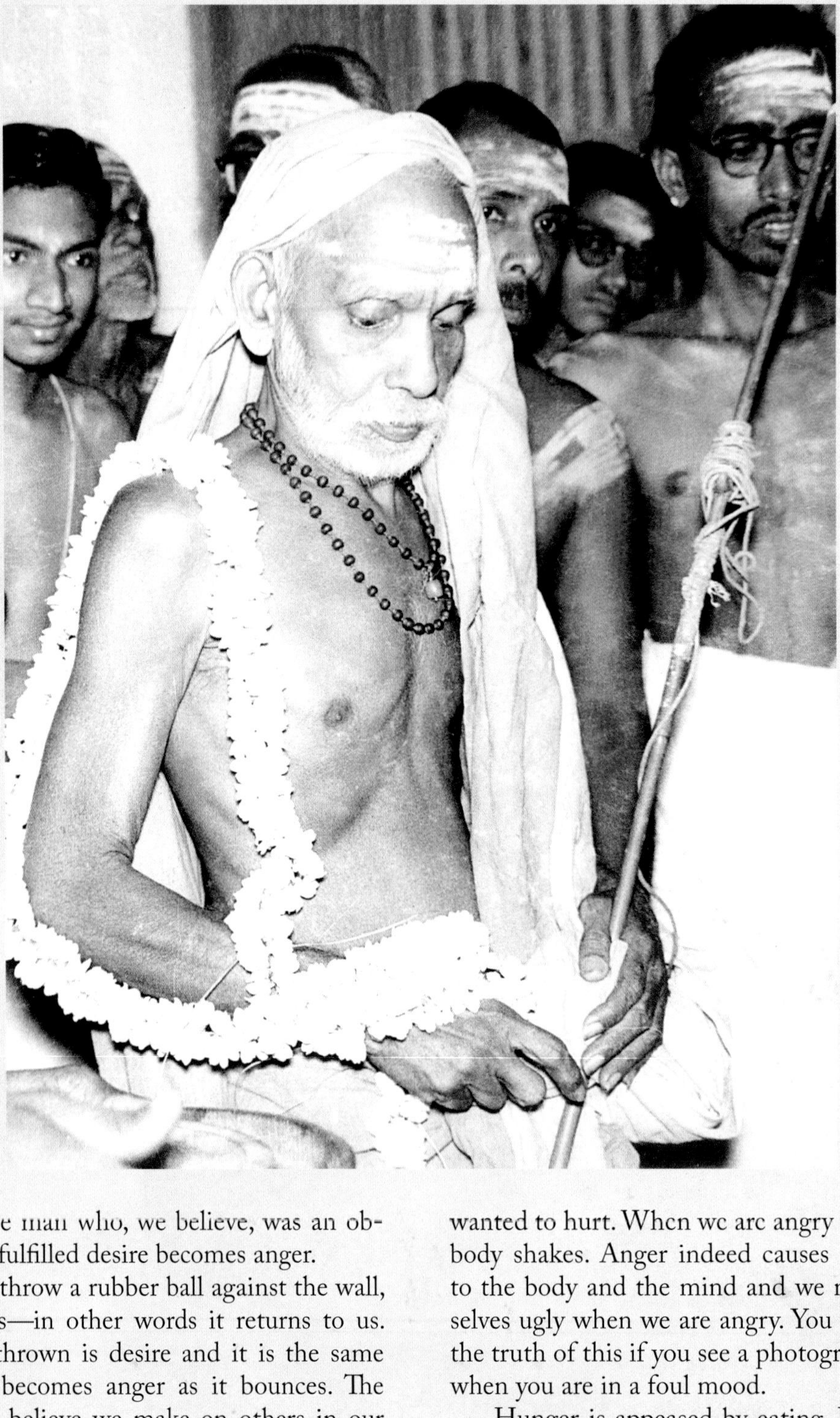

against the man who, we believe, was an obstacle. Unfulfilled desire becomes anger.

If we throw a rubber ball against the wall, it bounces—in other words it returns to us. The ball thrown is desire and it is the same ball that becomes anger as it bounces. The attack we believe we make on others in our anger is actually an attack we make on ourselves—and we are hurt more than those we wanted to hurt. When we are angry our whole body shakes. Anger indeed causes pain both to the body and the mind and we make ourselves ugly when we are angry. You will know the truth of this if you see a photograph taken when you are in a foul mood.

Hunger is appeased by eating. But is fire assuaged in the same way? You keep feeding it and it keeps devouring everything. Fire is bright but it chars all that it consumes. Or, in other words, it turns everything black. *Kāma* or desire is similar. It flares up like fire. The more it is fed the more it becomes hungry. Indeed *kāma* blackens our mind. When a desire is gratified there is joy for the moment, but soon it goes in search of more "food" and in the process we lose our peace of mind and happiness and become victims of sorrow and anger.

Sorrow and anger are two forms of unrequited desire. If we think that those who are a hindrance to the gratification of our desire are inferior to us, we turn our anger against them, and if we think that they are superior, all we do is to grieve within ourselves. Anger is packed with more evil power than even desire.

We must be extremely wary of this terrible sinner called anger. A little thought will convince us that we are not in the least qualified to be angry with anybody or to shout at anybody. We are even more guilty than those against whom we turn in our anger. We know this in our heart of hearts. Even if we are guiltless, before we rush to find fault with someone we must ask ourselves whether we would not have committed the offence we think he is guilty of were we placed in the same circumstances as he.

We must try our best to keep anger always at a distance.

Are We Worthy of Being Angry?

Our opponent is not likely to change his attitude towards us simply because we are angry with him. Instead, he might turn against us with greater venom. Hatred thus will be kept fuelled on either side. One must realize one's mistakes and try to reform oneself. We cannot congratulate ourselves if a person corrects himself fearing our anger. Also the change thus brought about in him will not be enduring. If we think that there is something wrong with a man we must try to correct him with love.

Why do people sin? The reason must be their mental condition and the circumstances in which they are placed. If we happen to be free from any guilt, it must be because we are more favored by circumstances. When you see a sinner you must pray: "O Ambikā, I too might have sinned like him. But in your mercy you did not give me the occasion to do so. Be merciful to him in the same way."

We must not be angry with a man even if he bears ill-will against us. Our innermost mind knows how far we deserve to be spoken ill of. It may be that the man who nurses bad feelings against us is doing so not because of any wrong done by us. We know, however, in our heart of hearts that the sins we have committed are indeed great. Such is our predicament that we must shed tears before Ambā (the *śakti* of Brahman), atone for our sins, and pray that they are washed away. In what way are we qualified to point an accusing finger at others?

Love and Sorrow

The purpose of human birth is to live a life full of love for all. No joy is greater than that of loving others. Amassing wealth, acquiring property, earning fame, bedecking oneself, give but transient pleasure, not any sense of fullness. The happiness that permeates our inner being is the happiness of loving others. When we love others we are not conscious of our suffering the physical exertion we make and the money we spend: indeed the joy of loving gives us a transcendent feeling. A life in which there is no love for others is a life lived in vain.

I said that when we love a person we forget our sorrows. But one day, at last, it may be that the object of our love itself becomes the cause of great sorrow. One day the person we love leaves us forever—or one day we will leave him forever. "O, he has left me forever"—"O, I am leaving him forever": we lament in this manner. We feel disturbed when we realize that all the happiness that love gave us has at last proved to be a lie and ended in sorrow. "Is the final outcome of love then sorrow?" we ask ourselves in our agitation. The greater our love for a person the more intense our grief when he or she is separated from us forever. We may then even wonder whether a life without love, a life of selfishness or a life of insensibility would be better. One leading such a life will not be affected by being separated from the object of his affection.

A selfish or self-centered man, however, gathers only sin. Is it not a life lived without joy—a life lived without a sense of fullness—a life lived in vain, a life like that of a log of wood or stone?

[The problem then is:] Our love for others ends in sorrow. However, if there is no love there is no meaning in life. What is the solution to this problem? We must create such love as will never change, love that will be enduring. The object of our love must never become separated from us, never desert us. If there were such an object and if we devoted all our love to it we would never be separated from one another—there would be eternal bliss, everlasting fullness.

To explain, we must love the One Object that never changes. What is that Object? The *Paramātman*. The *Paramātman* will never be separated from us. Even if our life departs it will dissolve in the *Paramātman* and become one with him. Only that love is everlasting which is dedicated to him.

The question arises: If one is to love the *Paramātman* that never perishes, does it mean that we must not love anyone else, that we must not love others because they will perish one day? If our love for the Supreme Being keeps growing the truth will dawn on us that there is no one or nothing other than He. All those whom we loved, all those who caused us sorrow by being separated from us, they too will seem to us the imperishable Supreme Being. We must learn to look upon the entire universe as the *Paramātman* and love it as such. Our love then shall never be a cause of sorrow.

Even if it be that our love is not such as to embrace the universe with all its creatures as an expression of the *Paramātman*, we can learn to love with ease all those great men of Ātmic qualities as the *Paramātman*, so also our guru who is full of wisdom and grace. Sufficient it would be to love them and surrender to them. Through them the *Paramātman* will give us his blessings. When someone we love dies we should not grieve for him. We must console ourselves that only the body which was the disguise of the *Paramātman* has perished, that the one who was in that disguise has become united with the *Paramātman*. Our love then will be everlasting. We must first learn to have such love for *Īśvara* and for people of goodness, for men of God. Then, step by step, we must enlarge it to embrace all. In this way the purpose of our life will be fulfilled.

Love

True love knows neither reason nor motive. When do we love a man truly? When our affection for him is unchanging and unwavering—we love him even if he does not apparently move closely with us or does not seem to possess inward qualities or the capacity to bless us; we love him even when we do not have any selfish interest to be served by him. Does anyone possess such love? Yes, only One. It is *Īśvara*—He alone has such love.

God loves us for no reason. If He needed a reason He would not give us even a morsel of food. It is *Parameśvara* who forgives us all our misdeeds and protects us—and He is all love.

We must, to start with, learn to have disinterested love for an individual, that is, love that is not tainted by self-interest. Eventually, this love will permeate us, inspire our inner being, and we will then be able to enlarge it to embrace all. It is the teaching of the wise that we must have such love for our guru, love without any consideration of the fruits thereof. We must not look for any reason to love our preceptor. If we constantly "practice" to have such love for our guru we will be the recipients of his blessings. Our love for him will eventually grow into love that will encompass all. If our love is manifested in this manner there will be fullness, tranquility, and bliss.

The State and Religion

True Secularism

The rulers of today are of the view that secularism should be followed by the Government ... in respect of religion. They understand this to mean that the State will not be inclined to any particular religion.

It is necessary to point out that this is not correct and show what true secularism is. It is not that the State should be completely detached from all religions. On the other hand a State, instead of being supportive of a particular religion, should support all the religions. The State should support all religions with equal concern and help in their growth, without mutual ill-will.

Responsibilities of the State in Elevating the People's Mind

It is true that it is the important responsibility of the State to do all that is necessary for the health of the people and the improvement of the quality of their life through education, agriculture and other economic activities, to take care of internal and external security, etc. But more important than the physical health is the mental health. The State cannot discard it. A country where people are not mentally elevated cannot be called a country. Since it is religion that develops the mental health it is certain that the State has a part to play in nurturing religion.

We see in practice that no developmental activity relating to worldly life gives permanent benefit and happiness. This kind of development becomes purely temporary and in securing it there is great competition, etc. On the whole there is only loss of peace. Because of modern discoveries the luxuries of life keep increasing. We are never satisfied and keep chasing them all the time. If our life ends with such endless effort to increase physical comfort it will be pitiable, despite being endowed with the rational faculty. What is required is that we have to find the ways and means of making what is imperfect into the perfect one, to make the temporary pleasures of life into permanent bliss. Good conduct, the ways of *dharma*, devotion to God, and spiritual thinking provide the way for it.

Limitations of the Role of the State in Matters of Religion

When it is said that the State has a part to play one thing needs to be understood. The State has merely a share in nurturing faith in religions as a means to develop the mind. That means the State should not entirely take over the responsibility for religious affairs. It should not exceed the limits in discharging its share of responsibility. Therefore the State should not at all interfere in the rules and practices of religions.

Irrespective of whether the State adopts the secularism by which it equally patronizes all religions or the wrong type of secularism by which it keeps no connection with any religion, it should not make laws in furtherance of its social policies which are contrary to the rules laid down in religion. Even after adopting the wrong type of secularism by which the State is neutral to all religions, if it tries indirectly to interfere in the rules of religions, we cannot accept it. But if a government wants to make laws in accordance with its social policies and if such laws are contrary to religious rules it should follow the basic policy that it will disregard equally the rules of all religions and mete out justice to people.

Before making laws concerning any branch it is the duty of the government to consult those who have vast knowledge and experience in it and obtain their advice. For this purpose, there should be a committee of experts for each branch.

It is not necessary that the rulers should have knowledge in the field of religion. In fact they need not even be religious. Therefore it means that this branch is beyond the purview of the government's law-making powers.

Independent Body of Representatives of All Religions

As a result of the above concept it becomes necessary that the government should organize an independent and autonomous body for taking decisions on matters of religion and it should keep itself completely away from it. It is only on the recommendation of such a body that the government can make any law if need be.

The objective of this independent body is to draw plans and implement them to nurture devotion to God, thinking of the soul, love, truth, straightforwardness, service, humility, etc., which are common to all religions. Its chief function should be to instill these good qualities in the followers of all religions who have been indulging in mutual quarrel and between sections of the same religion. The government should provide financial assistance to these bodies, not only because the government has a role in elevating the minds of people but also because all sections of people have to remain united for the government to function in an atmosphere of peace.

Who are those who are fit to find a place in this body? They should be those great persons who have dedicated their life to the study of the scriptures of their religion and in following the *anushtānās* (spiritual practices) of their religion. In addition to such persons, those who have these qualifications and are also well versed in the conduct of worldly affairs, and who have a close relationship with the people and know their mind and attitude, should also be members. There should be no interference of the government in this field for making changes.

Religious Leaders Should Not Involve Themselves in Politics

We wish to say the same thing about the role of religious leaders. That is, religious leaders should never interfere in matters of governance.

To keep reminding the government that it should act to nurture religion, to express appreciation when the government acts in this manner, to boldly criticize it if it interferes in matters of religion—beyond this religious leaders should not have connection with the government. Mixing politics with religion is like destroying the very source where water is purified. Their attention should be restricted entirely to religion.

What the Government Gains by Nurturing Religion

As an added reason for government extending support to all religions, we wish to show that apart from the government having its share in elevating the minds of people, the government itself benefits by such elevation. Presently, the government has to spend a lot over policing, courts, etc., because many offences are committed in violation of law and order. Apart from the expenditure, the very function of maintaining law and order is a heavy burden. If a small portion of this money is spent on nurturing religion and all the religionists are enabled to carry out maintenance of their places of worship, making grants to *satsang* (literally, "the company of the true"; gatherings with spiritual persons) and to worthy individuals in the manner of the kings of olden times, people will get mentally elevated and offences will come down substantially as in olden times. When the opportunity for material enjoyment is on the increase and the desire of the people keeps increasing the need for the government to nurture religion gains greater importance.

When, due to modern science and revolutionary ideas there is a danger all over the world of spirituality being lost, and if human beings are not to become like animals, this kind of secularism has to be followed.

Selected Wisdom

Foreign critics of our Vedic religion fling at us the cheap gibe, "What a host of gods and goddesses you worship!" This charge of polytheism leveled against our religion is entirely wrong and is born out of ignorance of the fundamental teachings of the Vedas. The One God appears in the three forms of Brahmā, Vishnu, and Śiva, for a three-fold purpose, namely, creation, protection, and dissolution. One *murti* (manifestation in form) appears as three, and there is no question of any one of the three being superior or inferior to the other two. If Brahmā, Vishnu, and Śiva are One in essence, then, by the same token, all the gods of the Hindu pantheon are also One in the ultimate analysis. Then why this wrangling that one god is superior to the rest? Some assert that the deity they worship is alone the highest. To a man standing under the arch at one end of a bridge, all the other arches will appear smaller than the one under which he is standing. But we are aware that all the arches of a bridge are of the same span. Similarly, to the votary of a particular deity, all the other deities will appear inferior on account of his attachment to the deity of his choice. But the truth is that all deities are manifestations, in particular ways, of one God.

* * *

One important difference between other religions and ours is that while other religions speak of a direct relation between man and God, our religion speaks of a mediated relation established through transcendental deities, each presiding over a particular aspect of worldly and spiritual life.

* * *

However bad a man may be, all evil thoughts within him recede to the background in the presence of his mother. Similarly, in the presence of the Divine Mother all of us can get rid of our mental impurity. The genius of our ancients is responsible for conceiving the Mother of all creation as a virgin (*kani*).

The conception of Divinity as the Mother is unique and inspiring. In human relationship the affection of a mother for her child is unsurpassed. Similarly, the depth of the Divine Mother's love for Her devotees is unfathomable. The grace that flows from Her is spontaneous and irresistible.

* * *

We should all strive to cultivate lofty and noble sentiments, and, eschewing all bad and selfish thoughts, live in a spirit of devotion to God and love for fellow men. Human stature increases in proportion to the nobility of human thought and deed. The spirit of selfless service, the readiness to sacrifice, devotion to God, and love for and goodwill towards all, and hatred for none, are the outcome of a highly developed mind, which goes by the name of culture.

* * *

Kingship has given place to democracy and therefore it has become the duty of the people themselves to preserve the treasures lying imbedded in our *śāstras* (scriptures). Instead we are frittering away our energies in linguistic and other controversies. This is a feature of our present-day life, which is very sad to contemplate. We must realize the basic principles expounded by our *śāstras* and model our lives accordingly. The only lasting thing is our endeavor for the elevation of soul. Realizing this, let us conduct ourselves in the proper manner.

No doubt, it is to some extent desirable, in this world, for a man to earn a name and fame and also material wealth. All these things come to some people unasked. Others do not get them, however much they may try. But these things do not attach themselves to us permanently. Either we leave them behind, or they desert us in our own life-time. Therefore, name, fame, and wealth are not objectives for which we should consciously strive with all our energy. What we should aspire and strive for is a life free from sin.

There are two aspects to this freedom from sin. One is absolution from sins already committed (*papa nasam*) and the other is non-commission of sins hereafter, by purifying our mind and making it free from evil thoughts (*papa budht*). The former can be achieved by absolutely surrendering oneself to God, realizing that He alone is our Savior, that nothing happens without His knowledge, and that whatever happens to us, good or bad, is by His will and only for our ultimate good. Resigning oneself to the dispensation of God is the essence of absolute surrender or *saranagati.* We will be free from evil thoughts hereafter only by *bhakti* or devotion, that is to say, by devoting every free moment of ours to His thought or repeating His names or listening to His glories.

While *saranagati* helps to "write off" past sins, *bhakti* alone will keep our minds away from sin. The heart has to be kept clean through *bhakti* so that the full effect of His presence there may be realized. In the ultimate analysis, surrender and devotion are the two facets of the same thing. In this life, all householders are engaged in various occupations necessary to maintain themselves. While so engaged, their minds will be concentrating on their work. But it is during their leisure that their minds are likely to go astray. This leisure must be utilized in developing *bhakti,* through various processes like *nāma japa* (repeating God's name), *satsanga* (keeping holy company), *satkathasravana* (listening to Lord's glory), *nooja* (worship), etc. The idea is to somehow keep our thoughts engaged on God. We should have no occasion to commit sin through mind, eyes, ears, and speech. Even when we make any supplications in our prayers, it should be in a spirit of detachment, namely, with the realization that nothing is unknown to Him and with a feeling, "Let Him do with us as He pleases". Let us, in this way, strive to pursue the path of surrender and devotion, and earn the grace of God.

* * *

True *bhakti* or devotion is that condition of a devotee's mind when it is unable to bear even a moment's separation from the shelter of God, and when even if it is forcibly withdrawn from that shelter, by force of circumstances, it struggles and rushes back and attaches itself to God, like a needle to a magnet.

* * *

A person may have everything that contributes to happiness, and yet, if he has not developed the proper frame of mind, he cannot be happy and contented. When his mind is a slave to discontent, anger, and envy, he cannot have peace and happiness. Like water kept in a leaky pot, everything he has will prove useless to him. Therefore, we should first of all seek God's help to cleanse our minds of all passions and impurities.

* * *

Fasting and other forms of discipline create a proper atmosphere for self-control; but complete self-control can be acquired only through the grace of God. Real control over the mind comes with the realization that everything, including oneself, is not other than God. With the dawning of the realization a person's senses cease to be attracted by external objects, his mind does not run away with his sense-organs, and he maintains his mental equipoise even under the most trying circumstances.

* * *

While desire fulfilled leads to further desire, desire frustrated turns into anger, like the rebound of a ball thrown at a wall. A person in the grip of desire or anger loses his reasoning power and consequently all his actions will be in the wrong directions. When desires become subordinate to the mind, the mind begins to dwell upon the *Ātman* undisturbed and a person steeped in the contemplation of the *Ātman* realizes the Supreme.

* * *

An ailment should be regarded as an opportunity to forget our normal physical wants and to contemplate on God. In that way, we can learn to do our routine duties in a spirit of dedication to God.

* * *

Each one of us is fond of certain things in life, and the liking develops into *rāga*, attachment or affection. When the things or persons we like part from us, or we part from them at the end of life's journey, we are afflicted with grief. Death forcibly separates us from the objects of our attachment, resulting only in grief all round. We must develop the capacity to leave this world without regret when death knocks at our doors. How this is to be achieved is the problem of life. We should strive to convert all our worldly achievements and resources into the currency *dharma,* so that we can carry with us this *dharma,* when the call comes to quit this world.

* * *

God is fullness, the All. There is no other to Him. He is the All without a second. That is *advaita* (non-duality). But mere intellectual comprehension of it is not enough. It must be realized as a fact in one's own experience. For such realization the grace of God is a prerequisite. We begin with a feeling of distinctness from God. The predicament of worship is one of duality of Deity and devotee. But even then the devotee does not feel that God is external to him and to the Universe; he has the consciousness that God is immanent in himself and in every particle of the world, indwelling everywhere and in everything, however min-

ute. Our duty is to worship Him in this way with devotion, and if we do so, He reveals His true nature to us.

* * *

A true *jnānin* (person following the path of knowledge) creates an atmosphere of detachment and holiness around him and draws innumerable people towards him. Such great *jnānins* have arisen in the world, from time to time, no matter what religion they professed. All these prophets and saints proclaimed the same Truth, each in his own way, and if they happened to come back to life now and meet together, there would be perfect unity in their messages. It is the followers that have put into their mouths more than what they said and wrangle with others, freezing the original teachings, mangled in their hands into institutional forms, which foster narrowness and bigotry.

* * *

Realization of the self as non-different from *Brahman* (the Transcendent Unity of God) is Supreme Bliss. That *Brahman* alone is real and the world has no reality in its own right apart from *Brahman* is the teaching of Śri Sankara.

* * *

We should employ even the few minutes of leisure we may be able to snatch in between jobs in the thought of God or in reciting His *nāma* (name).

* * *

Many God-saturated saints were not content by invoking God by one name only. They speak of Him having a thousand names (*per aayiram*), a thousand signifying innumerable. The lesson to be drawn from the foregoing is that the same Supreme Being appears in diverse forms, as we conceive Him to shower His grace in the manner we invoke it. We do it by *mantra* (a Divine formula) and *japa* (recitation of a *mantra*) which are sound waves having the power to transform the selves into the form of the *murtis* (sacred statues) whose *mantras* they are. If we continuously chant the *mantra* into which we are initiated, the Supreme *Paraśakti* (Mother-Power Supreme) will shower Her grace on us.

Notes

The Vedic Religion: Introductory

[1] The reference is to the *Katha Upanishad.*

[2] The reference is to the *Māndūkya Upanishad.*

The Vedas

[1] Rudra is the destructive manifestation of Śiva.

[2] This story is in the *Taittiriya Samhitā.*

[3] In *Advaita* the *Ātman* is identified with the *Brahman* or the *Paramātman.*

[4] The comment is in his *Mānisa-Pancaka.*

[5] *"Vedo nityam adhīyatām taduditam karma svanusthīyatām."*

[6] Specifically, the *Samhithās* and the *Brāhmanas.*

[7] This first *mahāvākya* occurs in the *Aitareya Upanishad* of the *Rigveda.*

[8] The second *mahāvākya* comes from the *Brihadāranyaka Upanishad* of the *Yajurveda.*

[9] This *mahāvākya* is from the *Chāndogya Upanishad* of the *Sāmaveda.*

[10] The fourth and final *mahāvākya* is from the *Māndūkya Upanishad* of the *Atharvaveda.*

[11] The *Sopana Pancaka* contains the sum and substance of Śankara's teachings.

[12] A related term, *upanayana* may be interpreted in two ways: leading a child to his guru; or leading him to the *Brahman*. Similarly, the term *Upanishad* could also be understood in the above two senses.

[13] Other *ācāryas* in the school of *Vedānta* are Rāmānuja, Madhva, and Śrikantha (the *ācārya* of *Saiva-Siddhānta*).

[14] The Upanishads are not in the form of *sūtras*; yet for the Vedāntic system they must be regarded as having the same "place" (or force) as the *sūtras.*

[15] Since Vyāsa dwelt under the *badarī* tree (jujube) he came to be called "Bādarāyana" and his work became well known as *Bādarāyana-sūtra.*

[16] Since it is an inquiry into those Upanishads which form the latter part of the Vedas, the *Brahmasūtra* is called *Uttaramīmāmsā.*

[17] The *Kena Upanishad* is also called the *Talavakāra Upanishad.*

[18] The basis for this quote is the *Chāndogya Upanishad* (8.12.1) which is part of the *Śruti.*

[19] These quotations are from the *Chāndogya Upanishad.*

[20] *"Dūrāt dūre antike ca,"* says the *Śruti* (Farther that the farthest, nearer than the nearest).

Nyāya (Science of Reasoning)

[1] *Nyāya* (science of reasoning) also does not lead to the *Lokāyata* system.

Purānās (Traditional Stories)

[1] "*Satyam vada*".

[2] "*Dharmam cara*".

[3] This is the story of Dharmaputra [Yudhisthira].

[4] "*Mātr-devo bhava*" and "*Ptir-devo bhava*".

[5] *Itihāsam = iti-hā-asam* ("it happened thus"). The *hā* in the middle means "without doubt", "truly". So an *itihāsa* means a true story, also a contemporary account.

[6] A *Purānā* must have five characteristic features—(*laksanas*). The first is *sarga* (creation of the cosmos); the second is *prati-sarga* (how eon after eon it expanded); the third is *vamśa* (the lineage of living creatures beginning with the children of Brahmā); the fourth is *Manvantara* (dealing with the ages of the 14 Manus, forefathers of mankind during the 1,000 *caturyugas*); and the fifth is *vamsānucarita* (genealogy of the rulers of the nation including the solar and lunar dynasties). In addition, there are descriptions of the earth, the heavens, and the different worlds.

[7] Of the *Rāmāyana* it is said: "As the Supreme Being, who is so exalted as to be known by the Vedas, was born the son of Daśaratha, the Vedas themselves took birth as the child of Vālmīki [in the form of the *Rāmāyana*]."

The Forty _Samskāras_ (Actions that Purify)

[1] The forty *samskāras* are set forth in the *Kalpasūtras*.

[2] The Buddha calls intense desire *tanha* in Prākruth.

Brahmacaryāśrama (Student-Bachelorhood)

[1] In the morning the dominant presence is that of Vishnu, at noon that of Brahmā, and at sundown of Śiva. So we must meditate on *Gāyatrī* in the morning as Vishnu personified, at noon as Brahmā personified, and at dusk as Śiva personified.

[2] This dispensation is called *sangavakāla*.

[3] The Gītā says "*Svakarmana tam abhyarcya siddhim vindati mānavah*".

[4] "*Patnīvatasya Agnihotram bhavati.*"

Marriage

[1] Neither is the procession called *janavāsam* approved by the *śāstras*, with all its glitter, taken out on the eve of the wedding as though it were an essential part of the ceremonies. In the past, when the bride and groom were very young, the wedding included functions to keep the couple in good cheer since they would perhaps have felt uncomfortable before the smoke of the sacred fire. There were elements of play like the procession. A big *pandāl* (wedding throne) too is not necessary.

[2] "*Kanyām kanaka-sampannām*".

[3] You cannot justify the acceptance of a dowry and other gifts on the pretext that they are given by the girl's parents on their own. This can lead to others also doing the same and cause a bad chain reaction. If the girl's parents give a dowry on their own, they will expect the same from the parents of their son's bride. You must refuse a dowry even when it is given voluntarily. The groom's parents spend on clothes, travel, etc., and expect the expenses to be "reimbursed" by the girl's parents. This is not at all justified. They must tell themselves: "Our son is getting married. Why shouldn't we ourselves spend for it? It is shameful to take money from someone else to buy our own requirements." Unfortunately, people think that they have certain rights and privileges as the groom's parents and fleece the bride's people by intimidating or browbeating them. Whether the dowry is given voluntarily or out of compulsion, it is money stolen. It is all a vicious circle that causes injury to society itself. We must somehow see to it that this evil system of dowry is scrapped.

Varna (Caste) _Dharma_ for Universal Well-Being

[1] "*Kalih sādhuh, Śūdrah sādhuh.*"

Dharmas Common to All

[1] *Ahimsā-pratisthāyām tatsannidhau vairatyāgah*—Yogasūtra, 2.35.

[2] *Vārigmanasyoh aikarūpyam satyam.*

[3] "*Satyam bhūtahitam priyam.*"

[4] This is called *go-grāsam* and this act is extolled in the *śāstras*.

Biographical Notes

HIS HOLINESS JAGADGURU ŚRI CHANDRASEKHARENDRA SARASVATĪ SVĀMĪGAL (1894-1994) was a renowned Hindu saint and mystic of the twentieth century. At the tender age of thirteen he was installed as the 68th pontiff in the line of succession of Ādhi Śankara in the Kāmakoti Pītham in Kānchi, South India. Throughout his eighty-seven year tenure as Jagadguru he exemplified in his simple and lofty life the essential worth of the *sanātana dharma* and exercised an enormous influence on all who came into contact with him. His very presence compelled admiration, awe, and conviction about the truth of the Vedas. At the time of his death at age 100, His Holiness was one of the most beloved and honored spiritual figures of the twentieth century in India. More than 6,500 pages of his oral discourses have been recorded, transcribed, and translated into English.

ŚANKARA (c. 509-c. 477 B.C.) was one of India's greatest saints and leading philosophers. He was born into a Brahmin family in Kāladi on the coast of Malabar, South India, and died in Kedārnāth in the Himalayas. At age eight he became a *sannyāsin*, or renunciate, and began to wander throughout India, taking as his guru Govindapada, the disciple of Gaudapada. He engaged in several public debates with leading teachers of rival philosophical schools, invariably defeating them and establishing the influence of the school of *Advaita* (or non-dual) *Vedānta*. Śankara founded several *pīthas* in order to revive the *sanātana dharma* and spread the teachings of non-dualism. The *pīthas* each possess a revered chain of spiritual transmission that exists to this day in the form and function of the *Śankarāchāryas*, or Śankara teachers, of which Śankara is the first (*ādhi*) and most eminent. Śankara, which means "he who brings blessings", displayed such remarkable wisdom and holiness during his lifetime that he is widely considered as an incarnation of Śiva.

MICHAEL OREN FITZGERALD is the author and editor of a dozen books on world religions that have received eleven prestigious awards. Eight of his books and two of his documentary films are used in university classes. Fitzgerald has taught Religious Traditions of the North American Indians in the Indiana University Continuing Studies Department and holds a Doctor of Jurisprudence from Indiana University. He has spent extended periods of time visiting traditional cultures and attending sacred ceremonies throughout the world. Fitzgerald and his wife live in Bloomington, Indiana.

ARVIND SHARMA received a Ph.D. in Sanskrit and Indian Studies from Harvard University in 1978 and was the first Infinity Foundation Visiting Professor of Indic Studies at Harvard University. He later succeeded Wilfred Cantwell Smith to the Birks Chair of Comparative Religion at McGill University in Montreal, Canada. He has published over fifty books and five hundred articles in the fields of comparative religion, Hinduism, Indian philosophy and ethics, and the role of women in religion. Often cited as an authority on Hinduism, amongst his most noteworthy publications are *The Hindu Gita: Ancient and Classical Interpretations of the Bhagavadgita*, *The Experiential Dimension of Advaita Vedanta*, *The Study of Hinduism*, and *A Guide to Hindu Spirituality*.

Glossary and Index

Iśvāra-bhakti: devotion to the personal God. 123
itihāsas: the two great Hindu epics, the *Rāmāyana* and *Mahābhārata*. 69, 70

jagat: the world; existence. 54
japa: silent repetition of a Divine formula or *mantra*. 5, 93, 113, 140
jāti: a sub-division of caste. 19, 101, 109, 110
jihād (Arabic): holy war. 8
jīvan-mukta: a person liberated in the embodied state itself. 63, 87
jīvan-mukti: deliverance or liberation in the embodied state; attaining enlightenment.
jīvātman: the individual self, or soul. 49
jnāna: spiritual knowledge, wisdom, enlightenment. 49, 51, 52, 55, 57, 61, 63, 65, 70, 85, 113, 116
jnānakānda: the latter part of the Vedas dealing with knowledge of the Self. 55, 61
jnāni: one who has attained *jnāna*. 49, 58, 59

Kali yuga: the iron age. 44, 106
kāma: desire; one of the four goals of life, along with pursuit of material acquisitions (*artha*); right conduct (*dharma*); and liberation (*moksha*). 39, 64, 95, 96, 97, 129
karma: the chain of cause and effect in action. 14, 16, 22, 52, 55, 57, 58, 87, 89, 95, 96, 97, 113, 117
karmakānda: the first part of the Vedas dealing with ritual work. 52, 55, 60, 61
Kartā: God as Creator. 120
kshānti: patience. 79
Kshatriya: a person of the warrior caste. 83, 101, 109
Krishna: the eighth incarnation of Vishnu; a central figure in the epic *Mahābhārata* and the Bhagavad Gītā. 2, 5, 8, 13, 45, 55, 57, 58, 63, 74, 103, 113, 129
krodha: anger. 64, 129
Krutha yuga: the golden age. 44

līlā: the Divine play; the sport of the Supreme Being. 73

Mahābhārata: the "great epic of the descendants of Bhārata", consisting of 106,000 verses in eighteen large chapters; attributed to Vyāsa. 69
mahāpralaya: the apocatastasis; the return of all things to the Self; the great deluge. 89
Mahāśakti: literally, the "great power"; the consort of Śiva; a personification of the "energy" emanating from *Brahman*. 62
mahāvākyas: literally, "great sayings"; the four "great sayings" from the Upanishads proclaim the identity of the individual self with *Brahman*. 52
mangala: what is auspicious. 79, 80
mantra: a Divine formula; a sacred phrase used in methodic invocation. 5, 6, 13, 14, 30, 31, 32, 33, 34, 35, 36, 45, 46, 48, 49, 52, 65, 79, 83, 85, 89, 91, 92, 93, 94, 95, 109, 140
Manu-smriti: the law book of Manu; also called the *Mānava Dharmaśāstra*. 123
Māyā: cosmic illusion. 70, 113
moksha: deliverance; liberation from the cycle of birth and death. 63, 65, 87, 96
murti: manifestation in form; also, sacred image. 140

nādi: blood vessel; nerve. 46, 48, 49
naishtika brahmacārin: lifelong student-bachelor. 86
nāma: name. 5
nāma japa: repeating the name of God; invocation. 138
namāz (Persian): Islamic prayers. 1
Nirguna Brahman: the Divinity without attributes; the Ultimate Reality or Supreme Principle. 89
nooja: worship. 138
nyāya: logic; the science of reasoning. 66, 141

pāpa: sin. 83
Paramātman: the supreme Self; the transcendent Unity of God. 1, 5, 6, 7, 8, 13, 14, 16, 32, 33, 44, 45, 46, 49, 51, 52, 55, 58, 61, 63, 73, 79, 87, 89, 103, 111, 113, 114, 117, 132, 140
Parameśvara: literally, the "transcendent Lord". 83, 127, 132
Paraśakti: the highest aspect of the Divine Mother. 140
paropakāra: helping others. 111
pītha (*peetha*): a seat of religious and spiritual authority. 29
prayoga: the proper procedure of rites. 30, 36
pūjā: ritual worship; daily offering rites. 39, 75, 77, 107, 111, 113, 117
punya: virtuous action. 2, 5
Purānās: traditional myths or stories of the gods. 40, 70, 71, 73, 74, 75, 82
pūśāri: one who performs *pūjās*. 70

rāga: attachment; affection. 139
rāja: king. 70
rajas: the active, expansive tendency; one of the three fundamental qualities, or *gunas*, of which the world is composed. 55. See *sattva* and *tamas*.
Rāmāyana: the oldest epic in Sanskrit literature telling the life story of the *avatāra* Rāma and his wife Sītā; attributed to the sage Vālmīki. 69, 70, 75, 123, 141
risis: ancient seers to whom the Vedas were revealed. 13, 40

sādhanā: spiritual practices leading to the mastery of the yogic paths. 120
Saguna Brahman: the Divinity with attributes; *Īśvara* or the personal God. 87
śakti: literally, "force, power, energy"; the consort of Śiva; the personification of the force or energy radiating from *Brahman*. 131
samādhi: absorption in the Infinite; a state of consciousness lying beyond waking, dreaming, and deep sleep. 55, 114

sāmānya dharma: universal code of conduct incumbent on all Hindus; includes: non-violence, truthfulness, cleanliness, control of the senses, non-acquisitiveness, devotion to *Īśvara*, trust in one's parents, and love for all creatures. 21, 124. See also *viśēsha dharma*.
samāvartana: returning home after completing study at the home of the guru. 85, 86, 95
samsāra: the cycle of birth and death. 65, 116
samskāras: rites and rituals that purify. 82, 83, 84, 86, 89, 93, 94, 95, 97, 141
sanātana dharma: the eternal religion. 6, 11, 14
sandhyāvandana: morning, noon, and evening prayers. 1, 89, 91, 92, 93, 120
sannyāsa: renunciation. 19, 52, 85, 87, 87, 96
sannyāsin: an ascetic who has renounced the world. 16, 52, 79, 86, 87, 89, 97, 124
saranagati: surrender or resignation to the will of God. 138
śāstras: scriptures. 13, 26, 35, 39, 40, 44, 46, 48, 66, 75, 76, 77, 85, 87, 91, 95, 97, 100, 101, 105, 106, 109, 113, 113, 114, 117, 141
satkathasravana: listening to the stories of the Lord's glories. 138
satsanga: holy company. 138
sattva: the pure, ascending tendency; one of the three fundamental qualities, or *gunas*, of which the world is composed. 55, 124. See *rajas* and *tamas*.
satya: truthfulness. 80, 120
saucha: purity, cleanliness. 79
siddhi: perfection; perfect ability; also psychic powers that appear as by-products of spiritual evolution. 33
Śiva: the destructive aspect of the Divinity. 19, 44, 66, 70, 71, 137, 140, 141
smriti: literally, "recollection, tradition"; scriptural texts that are traditional commentaries on the Vedas, including the *Dharmaśāstra*, *Rāmāyana*, and *Mahābhārata*. 123
Śruti: divinely revealed scripture; the Vedas. 45, 140
stthaanu: the stable one; one who remains unaffected by the temporal and changing things of the world. 121
Sūdra: a person who carries out the lowest of the tasks in the occupational division of the society. 84, 93, 101, 106, 109
svara: tonal variation; proper accentuation. 45
swami (*svāmi*): a title of respect for spiritual teachers and holy personages; also the lord. 2

tamas: the dark, descending tendency; one of the three fundamental qualities, or *gunas*, of which the world is composed. 55. See *sattva* and *rajas*.
Tretā yuga: the silver age. 44
trishnā: thirst; desire. 81

upakāra: extending help. 111
upākarma: first step for a young boy to become a Vedic student. 30
upanayana: the ceremony of initiating a youngster into Vedic study. 83, 84, 85, 89, 93, 97, 140
Upanishads: literally, "to sit down near to", i.e., to receive instruction from the guru; the final portion of the Vedas containing the *jnānakānda* or doctrine on the knowledge of the Self; forms the principal basis of the *Vedānta*. 19, 34, 52, 54, 55, 57, 58, 61, 63, 65, 79, 100, 140
upāsana: devotion, worship. 113

Vaiśya: a person of the merchant caste. 107, 109
vānaprastha: the stage of life in which the householder moves to the forest to pursue spiritual practices. 19, 87
varna dharma: caste system; comprised of priests (Brahmins); warriors (*Kshatriyas*); merchants/craftsmen/peasants (*Vaiśyas*); and those who carry out the lowest of the tasks in the occupational division of the society (*Sūdras*). 16, 19, 22, 25, 26, 109
varnaśrama dharma: the code of conduct (*dharma*) associated with a particular stage of life (*āśrama*) and a particular caste (*varna*). 16, 41
Vedānta: literally, the "concluding portion of the Veda"; the Upanishads, from which derive the three major philosophical schools of *Vedānta*: (1) *Advaita Vedānta* (non-dualism) associated with Śankara; (2) *Vishishtādvaita Vedānta* (qualified non-dualism) associated with Rāmānuja; and (3) *Dvaita-Vedānta* (dualism) associated with Madhva. 37, 52, 54, 55
videhamukta: a person delivered or liberated at death. 87
vidyā: learning. 85
vihāra (Pali): a Buddhist monastery; a residence for meditation. 7
viśēsha dharma: special code of conduct applicable to a caste. 21. See also *sāmānya dharma*.
Vishnu: the sustaining aspect of the Divinity. 19, 44, 66, 70, 71, 97, 137, 141

yajna: sacrifice; religious duty involving the sacrificial fire. 48, 49, 59, 61
yoga: literally, "joining, uniting"; any of a number of spiritual paths that lead to union with the Divinity. 32, 35, 63, 113, 117, 120, 123
yuga: an age; four *yugas* make up a *caturyuga*. 44, 107

Titles on Hinduism by World Wisdom

A Christian Pilgrim in India: The Spiritual Journey of Swami Abhishiktananda (Henri Le Saux)
by Harry Oldmeadow, 2008

The Essential Śri Anandamayi Ma: Life and Teachings of a 20th Century Indian Saint,
by Alexander Lipski and Śri Anandamayi Ma, 2007

The Essential Swami Ramdas: Commemorative Edition,
compiled by Susunaga Weeraperuma, 2005

The Essential Vedānta: A New Source Book of Advaita Vedānta,
edited by Eliot Deutsch and Rohit Dalvi, 2004

A Guide to Hindu Spirituality,
by Arvind Sharma, 2006

Introduction to Hindu Dharma: Illustrated
by the Jagadguru His Holiness Sri Chandrasekharendra Saraswati Swamigal,
Sankaracharya of Kanchi, 2008

Lamp of Non-Dual Knowledge & Cream of Liberation: Two Jewels of Indian Wisdom,
translated by Swami Sri Ramanananda Saraswathi, 2003

Paths to Transcendence: According to Shankara, Ibn Arabi & Meister Eckhart,
by Reza Shah-Kazemi, 2006

Timeless in Time: Sri Ramana Maharshi,
by A.R. Natarajan, 2006

Tripura Rahasya: The Secret of the Supreme Goddess,
translated by Swami Sri Ramanananda Saraswathi, 2002

Unveiling the Garden of Love: Mystical Symbolism in Layla Majnun & Gitagovinda,
by Lalita Sinha, 2009